The Little iBook Book

John Tollett

and Robin Williams

D1457053

Peachpit Press
Berkeley · California

Part III   On the Road   141

8 Before You Leave Home 143

How Important Is It? 144
Help for Mobile Connecting 144
Digital Phone Lines in Hotels 145
Beware Reverse Polarity 146
Do You Have Enough Cable? 146
These are Always Useful 146
Will you Need to Manually Dial for your Modem? 147
Pocket Phone 147
Pay Phones 147
Surge Protector 148
Local Access Numbers all over the Country 148
Calling Cards 148
Use the Location Manager 149
International Travel 152
International Power Plugs 152

9 Connecting on the Road 153

Why Travel with your iBook? 154
Planning Ahead 154
In the hotel room 156
Getting through the hotel switchboard 156
Using DialAssist 157
Back at the ranch . . . I mean hotel 159
Pick up a fax online 159
Use an Internet cafe 160
Check your other email accounts while on the road 160
Use an 800 access number to connect 160
Oh no, reverse polarity! 160
Fax from a pay phone 161
What to do about low-quality phone lines 162
Use a Smart Office at the airport 162
Send a file to Kinko's for hard copy output 162
Email from the airplane 163
Ignore the dial tone and dial manually to email 163

10 Printing & Faxing on the Road 165

Printing on the Road 166
Faxing on the Road 168
Free Faxing with eFax.com 171
Free Voicemail 172

11 Connecting from Foreign Countries 173

Foreign Issues 174
Power Adapter 174
Hertz 174
Surge Protector 174
Power Plug 175
Telephone Connectors and Jacks 175
Tax Impulsing 176
Dial Tone 176
Reverse Polarity 176
Digital Phone Lines 176
Pulse Phone Lines 176
International Calling Cards 177
International Internet Accounts 178
Web-Based Email 178
Check the Number 178
Check for Surcharges 178
Cell Phone Connections Overseas 179
Use a Local ISP 179
Remote Access Configurations 179
To Sum it all Up 180

Part IV Extras 181

Extra iBook Tips 183

12

Power Conservation Tips 184
System Software Troubleshooting 186
Unreliable Modem Connections 186
Airline Travel 187
  Laptop Lane and Smart Offices 187
  Airport Security 187
  Pardon my French 188
  Invest in a Travel Bag 189
  Car Travel 189
Staying Informed 190
Emergency Resurrection 190

Accessories 191

13

Converter Cables and Adapters for Connecting Non-USB Devices 192
Resources 192
USB Hubs 194
Palm Computing Connected Organizers 194
USB Mice, Game Pads, and Joysticks 194
USB Scanners and Printers 194
Video Capture 194
External Microphone and Speakers 195
Batteries and Battery Chargers 195
USB Drives (floppy, hard, Zip) 195
Portable Surge Protector 195
USB Cameras 196
Compact Flash and SmartMedia Card Readers 196
Auto and Plane Power Adapters 196
Retractable Modem Cable 196

Glossary 197

14

iLove iBook

Even if you've never owned a Mac you've probably heard those silly rumors about how Mac users are obsessed with their computers. If you have owned a Mac before, you know the rumors are absolutely true, perhaps even understated. There have always been plenty of good reasons for Mac-user enthusiasm, devotion, and loyalty, and the iBook is only going to fan the flames.

This book doesn't explain everything about how to use the basic operating system on your iBook. If you're new to using a Macintosh, you can find extensive information about it and how to have power over it (OS 8.6 is installed on the iBook) in *The Little Mac Book, sixth edition*. And you can find plenty of really basic Mac information plus tutorials for some of the bundled software in *The Little iMac Book*.

Hey, I'm Url and iLove my iBook!

For many of you, the iBook may be your first laptop and you'll be tempted to take it with you everywhere, dreaming up ways to make use of it as you travel for business or pleasure. Go ahead and give in to those temptations because the iBook is going to change the way you travel and keep in touch.

The more you use your iBook, the more reasons you'll think of to take it with you. Our friend Dave Rohr is an avid bicyclist and has been a participant in the annual Biking Across Kansas event for the past 25 years. During the week-long ride, he updates the web site **(www.bak.org)** with photos and reports from that day's ride. Family members and friends keep up with the ride through the web site. Important messages for participants are emailed to the site and delivered by one of the event organizers.

An out-of-town graduation can be the perfect opportunity for a personal web site. Now the relatives don't have to wait five or ten years for you to get around to mailing the family-event photos. Put some web authoring software on your iBook, take a digital camera to the event, and upload the site the same day.

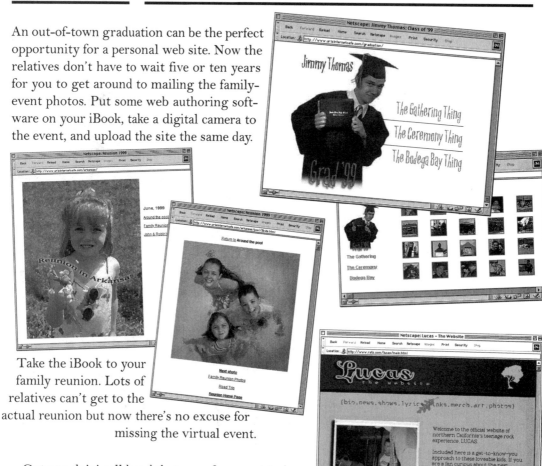

Take the iBook to your family reunion. Lots of relatives can't get to the actual reunion but now there's no excuse for missing the virtual event.

Got a rock 'n' roll band that your fans want to keep track of? Take your digital camera to your gigs to show folks what they missed, upload MP3 sound files so they can hear you anytime, and tell them who you are so they love you.

Got a deadline and you've missed FedEx? Use the iBook to send the project anywhere in the world, via the Internet. Need to keep in touch with family, friends, or associates while you travel? There's lots of travel tips included in this book. In fact, a large part of this book focuses on the challenges and techniques of connecting the iBook in various travel situations. The tips and suggestions included here can make a big difference in how successful your connection attempts are, especially when you're away from your home or office.

Just carrying around the cool-looking iBook is fun (Url says it's a babe magnet). We hope the information you find here adds to that fun and helps make your home- and mobile-computing more successful, giving you even more reason to say "iLove iBook."

with a smile, *John* and *Robin*

Part I At Home or Office

Perhaps you use your iBook at home, or maybe it's your office computer, or maybe you take it back and forth from home to office, school, tree fort, or clubhouse. Whatever you're doing with it, this first section will tell you about the features on the iBook that are different from what you may have experienced on another Mac. It covers the basics of the software packages that are already installed, the special features of the keyboard, how to get the iBook connected to the Internet, and how to set up your iBook to network and share files with other computers.

I'm at the office.

I'm not at the office.

I'm at the office.

I'm not at the office.

What Makes the iBook Different?

If you've seen an iBook, you know how different they look from the outside. But inside they are also a little different from desktop Macs. Oh, the basics are the same—you can open and close windows, organize files, customize your Desktop, use Sherlock to search your hard disk or the World Wide Web, etc. But because the iBook is portable, it's been juiced up with special features to make its portability as efficient and accessible as possible. It also has a number of other great features that make all-around computing more useful and fun.

If you are new to the Macintosh, you should first read *The Little Mac Book* to learn all about using every feature on your Mac and to get all the tips and tricks that even long-time users don't know. Even more basic is *The Little iMac Book*, specially written for brand-new users and those a little intimidated by a computer. Everything in that book will apply to your iBook computer. The iMac book includes tutorials to teach you how to use some of your software.

The iBook

The iBook represents a whole new level of power and mobility for computer users. The shock-resistant case, its wireless capabilities, and everything inbetween has been engineered to provide what all Mac users have come to expect: ease of use, super convenience, tons of fun, and big-time productivity. And the easiest-ever Internet connectivity.

Two of the iBook's add-on features, the wireless AirPort card and the AirPort Base Station, make laptop computing more mobile than ever before. If you didn't order your iBook with extra memory already installed, a RAM expansion module (memory chip) is easy to add. The new iBook keyboard incorporates features and functionality that have not been available before now. The iBook's energy management is improved, substantially increasing battery life.

Here's an introduction to some of the things that make your iBook more than your basic, run-of-the-mill laptop.

New Keyboard Features

See Chapter 3, The Keyboard, *for more details about these items.*

The iBook's new keyboard is full-sized and more versatile than previous keyboards.

♦ The **fn key** provides the F1–F6 keys and several other keys with extra features.

♦ The Fkeys from F7 through F12 are **user-defineable** — set them up to open often-used applications, documents, AppleScripts, or to access another disk on the network.

♦ Use the **fn key** and **Num Lock** to access a numeric keypad.

Read all about the new keyboard features in Chapter 3.

A **port,** or connector, is a place where you plug things into your computer. If you've worked on a desktop Mac, you might be surprised to find fewer ports on the iBook than you are accustomed to. If you know what a SCSI port, serial port, or ADB port is, well, you won't find them on the iBook. (And if you don't know what they are, so what because they're not here anyway.)

Ports

Input and output connectors (I/0)

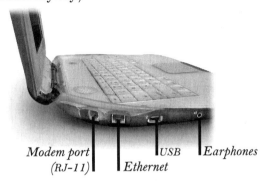

Modem port (RJ-11) | Ethernet | USB | Earphones

Your iBook has one **USB port** for connecting devices such as a hard drive, floppy drive, Zip drive, scanner, printer, mouse, keyboard, or digital camera. Because USB is a new technology, any device you want to attach to your iBook has to be what's called "USB-compatible."

USB port

Many people will tell you that any USB device will work on the Mac. Wrong. Make sure it is definitely compatible before you buy it and that it comes with any necessary drivers.

Since there is only one USB port, you'll need a USB hub if you want to connect more than one device at a time. Hubs are available with various numbers of ports, depending on how many devices you want to connect. A list of available USB devices is available at **guide.apple.com/usindex.html** and at **www.macintouch.imacusb.html.**

The **RJ-11 port** (the **modem port**) takes a standard RJ-11 phone cable (shown to the right) to connect the iBook's built-in modem to a phone line. You can also use a modem cable that has RJ-11 connectors.

RJ-11 modem port

The iBook also has an **RJ-45 Ethernet port** for connecting to a network, a cable modem, a DSL connection (Digital Subscriber Line), or another computer. An Ethernet connector looks very much like a standard phone jack connector, but it's a little bigger.

Ethernet port

The 16-bit **headphone jack** is where you can plug in your earphones.

Headphone jack

The **power port** is where you insert the AC adapter (the power plug that goes into the wall socket) to power your iBook. While it's plugged into the wall, the battery recharges at the same time. The battery recharges while you work, and it recharges even faster when the iBook is shut down (as long as it's plugged in).

Power port

Restart and Reset

Occasionally a computer will just go psycho and freeze up. Sometimes this happens because the settings in the computer hardware corrupt over a period of time, or it might be caused by static electricity, or even a collision of data inside the computer or wires. Strange behaviors may result, ranging from a freeze-up to a refusal to charge the battery.

If this happens, try the **restart** key combination:

♦ Hold down the Control and Command keys and push the Power key.

If that doesn't work, use the iBook's **reset button:**

♦ The reset button is the small paperclip-sized hole above the Power button at the top of the keyboard. Insert the end of a paperclip into the reset hole to reset the computer. Wait five seconds and start the computer again by pressing the Power button.

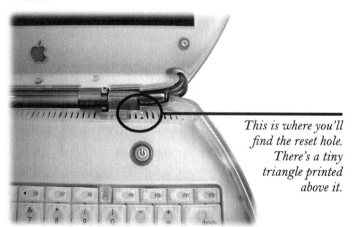

This is where you'll find the reset hole. There's a tiny triangle printed above it.

After you reset or restart this way, on startup you'll get a message box informing you that the machine was not shut down properly (like you weren't there when it happened?). You can avoid this sermon in the future by opening the General Controls control panel and unchecking "Warn me if computer was shut down improperly."

Your iBook, of course, has a trackpad instead of a mouse. You use your finger as a mouse. Be sure to check out the **Trackpad control panel** to adjust it to your liking.

♦ As with your regular desktop mouse, you can set the "speed." This doesn't refer to how *fast* your finger moves; it refers to how *far* you have to move your finger to make the pointer move across the screen. A "fast" tracking speed means you can move your finger a shorter distance across the pad to move the pointer across the screen. A "slow" speed means you have to move your finger farther to move the pointer. Experiment to see exactly how it works.

For regular work on your iBook, you might prefer a faster setting. If you work with graphics and want fine-tuned pointer movements, set the tracking speed slower.

♦ The "Double-Click Speed" can be changed if you find you're not fast enough with your finger. If you double-click too slowly, it will be interpreted by the computer as two single-clicks. If you find you're always double-clicking too slowly, set the speed slower so the computer understands two of your slower clicks is really a double-click.

♦ The last set of features is great. Check the "Clicking" box so you can tap directly on the trackpad instead of having to press the clicker that's directly below the trackpad. Same for "Dragging" and "Drag lock"—they allow you to drag with your finger on the trackpad instead of having to use two hands to drag (one to hold down the clicker and one to drag across the trackpad).

You might wonder why you even have a **Mouse control panel** on your iBook. It's because you can always add a mouse, which John greatly prefers to do.

Also, the "Mouse Tracks" feature applies to your trackpad movements as well! Experiment with the mouse tracks—it creates a "trail" of pointers that flow along as you move the pointer. This is great for teachers and presenters; it helps the class or audience follow the movements of the pointer across the screen.

The "Thick I-beam" can also be useful for presentation purposes, or even if you just want a more easily seen I-beam. (The I-beam is the cursor within text.)

Trackpad Control Panel

Mouse Control Panel

Energy Saver
Control Strip Module

You can enhance the portability of your iBook by maximizing the life of the battery. Press on the **Energy Saver control strip module** (the moon and stars icon, shown below) to open a popup menu with shortcuts for making quick changes to the energy conservation settings. The "Sleep Now" setting lets the system rest in a low-power mode, and while it rests it puts less drain on the battery.

This is the control strip typically found in the bottom left of your screen.

Energy Saver
control panel

To make more detailed modifications to the settings, use the Energy Saver control panel. In this control panel you enter settings that prolong battery life, and determine behavior for start up, shut down, sleep, and wakeup.

To open the Energy Saver control panel

♦ From the popup menu in the control strip (shown above), select "Open Energy Saver Control Panel."

♦ **Or** go to the Apple menu, slide down to "Control Panels," then choose "Energy Saver."

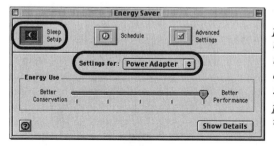

This is the control panel for adjusting the energy drain on the computer. You can set individual settings for using the power adapter or for using the battery.

Sleep Setup

The **Sleep Setup** mode shown above lets you choose different settings for when you use the iBook with the power adapter (plugged in) or with battery power. When you're plugged in, go for the "best performance;" when you're using the battery, be more "conservative" to maximize the battery life.

From the menu labeled "Settings for," select "Power Adapter." Using an AC power adapter (the power plug that goes into the wall) eliminates any energy concerns, so you can move the "Energy Use" slider all the way to the right toward "Better Performance," as shown above.

You can set separate sleep settings for the display (which just turns the screen dark) or the hard disk (which makes the system itself rest). Click the "Show Details" button and adjust the sliders as desired.

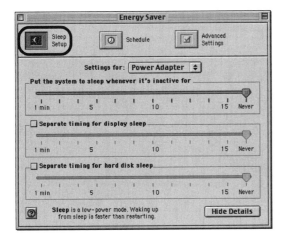

From the "Settings for" menu, select **Battery.** To maximize the life of your battery, move the "Energy Use" slider to the left toward "Better Conservation."

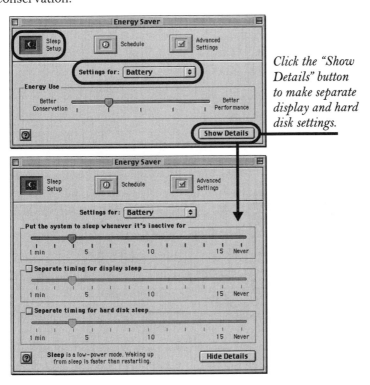

Click the "Show Details" button to make separate display and hard disk settings.

Schedule Click the **Schedule** button at the top of the menu. You can make your iBook start up at a certain time so when you walk in the door of your office or when you crawl out of your dorm-room bed, the computer is up and running. You can tell it to shut down at a certain time as well. And you can schedule its sleep patterns.

To schedule the iBook to start up or shut down automatically

1. Click the checkbox under "Schedule Options."

2. Set the controls to the desired day and time.

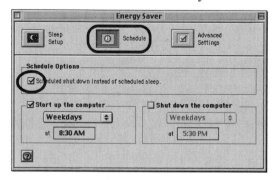

If you've scheduled a shut down, the iBook will notify you 5 minutes in advance so you'll have time to cancel if necessary. If you'd like an additional notification 15 minutes earlier, go to the Preferences menu and choose "Notification." Click the "Notify me" checkbox, and choose what type(s) of notification you want.

To schedule the iBook to sleep or wake up

1. Uncheck the checkbox under "Schedule Options."

2. Set the controls to the desired settings.

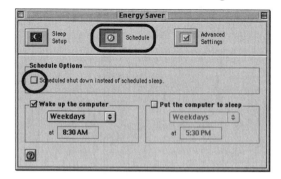

The **Advanced Settings** option offers even more options.

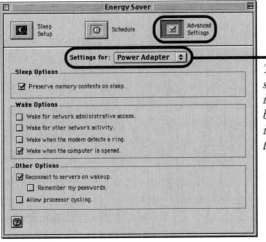

You can set separate settings for when the iBook is using the battery and for when it's plugged in with the power adapter.

♦ Check the box for "Preserve memory contents on sleep" under **Sleep Options** to save the contents of memory to your hard disk before the iBook goes to sleep. This will prevent the loss of any data you had open if the iBook loses power while sleeping.

♦ The **Wake Options** let you select situations when your iBook will wake from sleep. If you're connected to a network, you'll probably want to check at least the first two boxes: "Wake for network administrative access" allows network administrators access to your iBook, and "Wake for other network activity" allows someone to log in remotely to your iBook. In both cases, it could be yourself that you're granting access to, especially if you have a small home or office network. The "Wake when the computer is opened" option is handy when going through airport security because your machine will start right up.

♦ The **Other Options** enable you to "Reconnect to servers on wakeup," which is self-explanatory. "Allow processor cycling" switches the processor that runs the computer to a reduced power mode when the iBook is idle. When you're setting the Battery settings, you should check this box to help conserve battery power.

Important: *Virtual memory must be turned on in the Memory control panel for this to work; it's on by default, so if you haven't turned it off, don't worry about it.*

*If you check this option, **don't move your iBook** for at least 20 seconds after it goes to sleep! when the iBook has finished saving the contents to memory, you'll see the beacon light blink.*

The iBook has a **beacon light** located on the cover hinge: when the iBook goes to sleep, the beacon light slowly dims and brightens. Hmm. Sort of like a beacon. The light is visible with the cover open or shut.

**Sleep Mode
Beacon Light**

Replace the Battery If you need to replace the iBook battery, it's easy to do. This is what the battery itself looks like:

To replace the battery

1. Shut down the iBook.

2. Leave the AC power adapter plugged in, if power is available. This will preserve the contents of something called PRAM (pronounced *pee ram*), a special kind of memory that maintains certain settings in some control panels. If you don't have access to a power outlet, a small capacitor in the iBook will maintain the PRAM contents for about 20 seconds. That might not seem like much time, but it's actually twice as much as you need.

   If it takes longer than 20 seconds to change the battery, some of the control panel settings you've customized will return to their default settings. You'll have to change the control panel settings back to the way you want them after you've installed a charged battery. Especially check the Mouse and the Date & Time control panels, and choose your printer again.

3. Turn the iBook upside down.

4. You'll see two spring-loaded latch screws. Turn them about one-quarter turn counterclockwise and then remove the cover of the battery bay.

   Low-tech tip: The screw slots are so large that a quarter (25¢ coin) actually works much better than a screwdriver. Handier, too.

These are the latch screws.

5. Position the new, charged battery upside down so that the connector in the middle of the battery lines up with the connection in the battery bay, as shown below. The used battery is still in place at this point—what we're doing is lining up the new battery so as soon as we pull the used one out, the new one can slip right in.

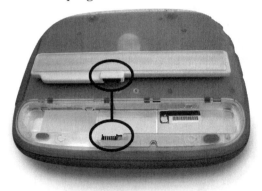

6. Pull on the plastic tab to remove the discharged battery.

7. Place the new, charged battery in the bay. You now have battery power and can replace the cover.

Easy Installation of RAM . The iBook comes with 32MB of RAM (Random Access Memory), which is a minimal amount of memory for most computer users today. If you didn't have extra memory installed at the factory, you can expand the iBook's memory by adding a RAM expansion card (memory chip) to the RAM slot underneath the keyboard. Compatible RAM modules are available in 32, 64, and 128MB capacities, to a maximum of 160MB total.

To install a RAM expansion card

1. Unplug the AC adapter (the power plug) and remove the battery (see the previous two pages for removing the battery).

   Caution! Always be cautious about static electricity when installing RAM or an AirPort Card. Work in a room without carpet because carpet builds up static electricity when you walk across it. And toss your cats out the door. Before you start, discharge any static electricity that may be present by touching something metal near you.

2. If you've been using the iBook, the interior may be hot. Allow 30 minutes after shutting down before you remove the keyboard.

3. Unlatch the keyboard: slide the two latches located to the left of the F1 and F9 keys (circled, below) toward the front of the computer.

   If the top part of the keyboard does not pop up, unlock it with a very small flathead screwdriver: the plastic tab to the left of the Num Lock key (F5 key) has a slotted screw in the middle of it (which is also the Num Lock light); turn the screw counterclockwise to unlock the keyboard.

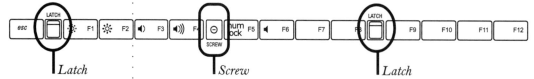

Latch   *Screw*   *Latch*

4. Slide the keyboard forward (toward the screen) just enough to disengage the small tabs at the front of the keyboard from the slots they're in. Lift the keyboard up and turn it upside down, resting it on the trackpad and palmrest of the iBook—the keyboard remains attached to the keyboard cable.

5. Touch a metal surface on the inside of the computer to discharge any static electricity you've built up in your body.

6. If an AirPort Card is installed, remove it: flip up the wire bracket, then pull on the card's pull tab to disconnect it from the connector (just under the front edge of the palmrest).

7. Under where the AirPort Card would be is the RAM shield, a solid piece of metal that covers the RAM slot. Remove the two screws on the right side of the RAM shield (circled, below) and lift the metal cover out of the computer.

8. Discharge any static electricity again by touching a metal surface inside the computer.

9. Insert the RAM expansion card into the RAM slot at a 30-degree angle, making sure the notch in the card lines up with the small tab in the expansion slot. Push the expansion card into the slot. If it doesn't go in easily, try pushing one side at a time. Push the card down flat until the two snaps on both sides of the card lock into place.

The white rectangle in this illustration outlines the inserted RAM module.

The circles show the location of the two screws that hold the RAM shield in place.

10. Replace the RAM shield and secure the two screws that hold it in place.

11. Reconnect the AirPort card, if you have one. Flip down the wire bracket.

12. Replace the keyboard by flipping it back over on top of the open compartment. Insert the tabs at the bottom of the keyboard back into the slots at the front edge of the palmrest. Pull back on the latches as you lower the keyboard and press it into position. Release the latches so they snap into their slots.

File Synchronization Control Panel

Basically, all this process does is replace one file with another. It does not truly "synchronize" files like the Palm's HotSync software does with its database documents.

But you might find this useful to coordinate files back and forth between your iBook and your desktop Mac.

The File Synchronization control panel is a tool to keep multiple files of a document current and updated. It's most useful if you often work on two different computers, or if two people using separate computers need to work on the same files.

You synchronize two files or two folders by creating a link between the two, determining the direction of the link, and updating the linked pairs whenever necessary. This is what the control panel looks like when you first open it:

First set up a network!

If you want to link and synchronize files or folders that are on different computers, you'll first need to establish a **network** connecting the two computers. See Chapter 5 for more about File Sharing.

Set up a link

To set up a link between two files or folders

Any two files that you link must have the same name and initially must be identical files. (Linked *folders*, however, can have different names.)

1. From the Apple menu, slide down to "Control Panels," then choose "File Synchronization."

2. In the dialog box, select a file to synchronize by double-clicking in the *left*-hand window. A dialog box appears that enables you to select a file or folder that you want to create a link to. Select the file or folder with a click, then click the "Select" button.

   Tip: Instead of double-clicking this box to select a file or folder, you may find it easier to just drag a file or folder from anywhere on your computer and drop it in the left-hand window.

   The selected file or folder icon appears in the left-hand window.

3. Next, double-click the *right*-hand window and choose another file or folder from another location or computer. Or, instead of double-clicking the right-hand box, drag a file or folder into it.

   Remember, the file you link to in the right-hand window must be named exactly the same as the file in the left-hand window, and they both must have originated from the exact same file!

By default, a linked pair is set for **two-way synchronization,** indicated by the two-way arrow linking the two windows. With two-way synchronization, changes in either file will be copied to the other. However, if both files have been changed since the last update, synchronization will not work anyway!

Determine the direction of the link

You can **change the link direction** to one-way in either direction by clicking the arrow between the two windows. A one-way link direction determines one copy of the file as the *master* file (or folder) and the other copy of the file as the *destination* file (or folder). Changes made to the *master* are copied to the *destination*. Changes made on the destination copy are *not* copied to the master file.

- ◆ Click the arrow once to turn it into a Left-to-Right link (master on the left, destination on the right).
- ◆ Click again to change the arrow to a Right-to-Left link (master on the right, destination on the left).
- ◆ A third click returns the link to a Two-Way link.

You can also set the link direction through the Synchronize menu that appears in the menu bar when the control panel is active. You have three choices: "In Both Directions," "Left to Right," and "Right to Left."

You can **update links** automatically or manually by choosing "Automatic" or "Manual" from the Synchronize menu.

Update (synchronize) linked pairs

- ◆ The "Automatic" option will synchronize the linked pairs whenever you open the File Synchronization control panel, using whatever link directions are set for each pair.
- ◆ The "Manual" option will not update links until you click the "Synchronize" button, giving you the opportunity to change link directions for any pair before updating.
- ◆ You can toggle between "Manual" updating and "Automatic" updating: hold down the Option key and click the link direction arrow.

Scan the files The Scan button starts a scan of the selected pair to determine if any files have changed. A scanning window appears that shows the names of files being scanned. This happens so fast the only practical purpose of that window is to assure you the scanning is in progress.

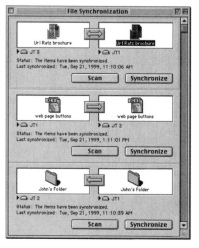

Click the "Scan" button to let the iBook check to see if and which files have changed.

To delete a link

♦ Select a linked pair by clicking on the file or folder. From the File menu, choose "Delete Pair." ***This does not delete any files or folders;*** it only breaks the link between them.

♦ Select multiple pairs for unlinking: hold down the Shift key as you select pairs, then chooose "Delete Pair" from the File menu.

♦ To break all links, choose "Select All" from the Edit menu before you choose "Delete Pair" from the File menu.

Set your preferences In Preferences (from the Edit menu) you can enable the synchronization of *folders* (not files) with different names. Check the box, "Let me synchronize folders with non-matching names."

Set alerts for certain conditions that may threaten the integrity of your file synchronization, such as a change in the destination file of a one-way linked pair. If you don't want to receive these alerts, uncheck the boxes under "Have File Synchronization generate an error if."

The Preferences dialog box also gives you several choices of what action to take when a synchronization error occurs.

The iBook battery charges in two hours when in Sleep mode. If the iBook is in use, charging takes four hours. A fully charged battery's life is six hours, although that could vary depending on the nature of the work you're having the iBook perform (word processing is not highly energy-consuming, but graphics and image processing are). Other factors that affect battery life are the settings you made in the Energy Saver control panel, as well as any external devices you've connected to the iBook. See Chapter 12 for energy-saving tips.

A Better Battery

If your iBook is plugged into a wall socket for power, you can tell at a glance if the battery is fully **charged** or not.

Battery charge indicator light

♦ A fully charged battery will make the power adapter port glow **green.**

♦ If the battery is in the process of being charged, the power adapter port glows **amber.**

If the iBook is using its internal battery for power, the power adapter port does not glow.

The two circular metal contacts located on the bottom of the iBook just below the Apple logo are **charging contacts.** The contacts are for connecting to iBook battery charging stations that can charge several iBooks simultaneously. Charging stations will be available from third-party developers for use in school or office settings where many iBook batteries need to be recharged at one time, eliminating the need to plug each iBook into a wall socket for recharging. The metal contacts are safe to touch, and accidental contact with other objects, including metal, won't harm the battery or the computer.

Battery-charging metal contacts

AirPort Base Station

This is an AirPort Base Station. Above you see the front of it, and below you see the back, where the ports are.

The **AirPort Base Station** and the **AirPort Card** (below) are optional items that enable wireless Internet connections and wireless networks for your home, school, or office. The Base Station costs around $300, and each AirPort Card costs around $99.

The process works like this: You connect the Airport Base Station to the Internet through its 56K modem or through some other Internet connection plugged into its Ethernet port. You install AirPort Cards in up to ten iBooks (or install wireless networking cards, like the Skyline Wireless PC Card from Farallon for $280, into other laptops). Then each of the ten iBooks can connect to the Internet without any cables at all—they use a wireless radio connection through the AirPort Base Station. In fact, the iBooks don't even have to be in the same room; they can be up to 150 feet away if indoors and up to 300 feet away outdoors.

The Base Station uses security software (specifically, forty-bit encryption and password-protected access) to insure privacy and security for the wireless network. If you buy an Ethernet crossover cable, you can connect the Base Station to another Macintosh desktop computer or to an Ethernet network. For more information, see Chapter 5.

AirPort Card

This is a wireless network card. It's small emough to fit in the palm of your hand.

The **AirPort Card** is a wireless LAN (Local Area Network) card that you can easily install in the iBook under the keyboard. This card enables your iBook to communicate wirelessly with other computers that are equipped with wireless LAN cards. With an AirPort card, you can have wireless access to the Internet, e-mail, or to an Ethernet network. This means you can transfer files, play multi-user games, and access any files from any computer in your network at blazing speeds. This technology doesn't depend on direct-line-of-sight between computers, so if you're in another room or on another floor, upstairs or downstairs, you can still connect to the wireless network if you're within 150 feet.

An iBook acts as a base station

If you don't have an AirPort Base Station, **an iBook itself will function as a base station (called an "access point") if you put an AirPort Card in it.** The AirPort card software enables the iBook to act as a bridge between wireless signals and a wired network. Up to ten other iBooks that have AirPort cards installed can wirelessly share the Internet or network connection of the iBook that has been designated as an access point.

There's more information about AirPort and wireless features in Chapter 5.

Software
on the iBook

Your iBook arrives with a wide variety of useful (and useless) software. Let's take a look at what each application offers you. Below is a list of the applications and a note about whether it's already installed on the iBook or if you need to use the CD-ROM that's included. The rest of the chapter provides more information.

Mac OS 8.6: The operating system that runs the computer. It's already *installed* for you. You also have a CD that contains the entire system in case you ever need to reinstall it.

AppleWorks: An "integrated software package" that includes a word processor, database, spreadsheet, paint program, draw program, and telecommunications program. *Installed.*

Palm Desk Organizer: Software to keep track of appointments, contacts, etc. *Installed.*

FAXstf: Software to fax anything on your iBook from anywhere in the world. *Installed.*

Netscape Communicator 4.61, Microsoft Internet Explorer 4.5: Browsers for the World Wide Web. You can also use them for email and newsgroups. *Installed.*

America Online 4.0: Online service. You can also use it for email, newsgroups, and to surf the World Wide Web. *Installed.*

EarthLink Total Access: Internet service provider; through EarthLink you can get email and surf the World Wide Web, using one of the browsers mentioned above. *Installed.*

Microsoft Outlook Express: Email software, if you have an Internet service provider. You can also use it to access newsgroups. *Installed.*

Bugdom: A very cute game. *Installed.*

EdView Internet Safety Kit: Software for parents to limit access to children or any other immature family members. *This is on a CD; you need to install it.*

World Book Encyclopedia: The traditional encyclopedia in multi-media format on CD. *Install part of it; insert CD to use.*

Adobe Acrobat Reader: Software that reads "pdf" files (Portable Document Format). Almost every software package on your computer and on the CDs has a manual that is saved in the .pdf format. Simply double-click one of these manuals and it will open in the Acrobat Reader, maintaining all of the original formatting and typefaces. *Installed.*

The rest of the chapter elaborates on these various pieces of software. Skip it or read it as you find it necessary.

Mac OS 8.6

The **operating system** is what runs your computer. The particular version that was installed on the iBook at the time we wrote this edition of the book is Mac OS 8.6. If you are new to the Macintosh and want to know all the details about every control panel, all the tricks in Desktop and application windows, how to customize the appearance of your Desktop, and much more, please see *The Little Mac Book, sixth edition.* We apologize, but it just wasn't possible to include all of that basic information in this book!

AppleWorks

As we mentioned on the previous page, AppleWorks is an integrated software package, which means it includes a word processor, database, spreadsheet, paint program, draw program, and telecommunications program. Because it is one package that includes all of these individual programs, each individual module is not quite as powerful as if you bought a separate application. For instance, the word processor is great, but it's not as powerful as a separate application like Microsoft Word that is devoted to just word processing. Likewise, the database module is great, but not as powerful as a separate database application like FileMaker Pro. For most people, though, the modules in AppleWorks are perfectly adequate. If you find you do outgrow one of the modules, then you can upgrade to a more expensive and expansive application; all of your documents you created in AppleWorks should open just fine in the newer and bigger application. If you are interested in learning AppleWorks, you'll find a simple tutorial for each module in *The Little iMac Book*, by Robin, or read *AppleWorks 5: Visual QuickStart Guide*, by C. Ann Brown (both from Peachpit) for all the details.

An amazing thing is going to happen when you start working with the Palm Desktop Organizer . . . you're going to be more organized than you ever thought possible. Even more amazing, it'll be easy and fun.

To install the Organizer, look in the Applications folder for a folder called "Palm Desktop." Look in that folder for the file called "Palm™ Desktop Installer." Double-click the installer icon and follow the directions.

Once you've installed the Palm Desktop Organizer software, a calendar icon appears in the menu bar at the top of the screen. Press on this icon to see your options, including a list of events, appointments, and tasks that have been entered for the current day.

This calendar icon will stay in your menu bar so you always have access to the Palm Desktop Organizer.

Choose "Open Palm Desktop" to launch the application and place the Palm Desktop toolbar (shown below) on the screen.

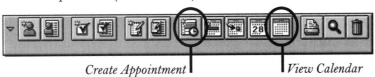

Create Appointment | *View Calendar*

As you mouse over the buttons in the toolbar, a tiny message box appears that describes the function of each button.

Palm Desk Organizer

Installing the Organizer

Palm™ Desktop Installer

Use the calendar

To use the calendar, click the **View Calendar** icon (shown to the left).

The calendar has three views, **Daily, Weekly,** and **Monthly,** labeled on tabs on the right side of the calendar. Click a tab to change the view.

This is the toolbar button to "View Calendar."

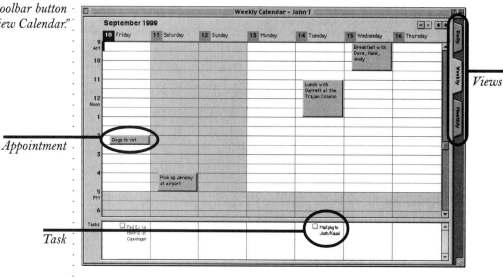

Views

Appointment

Task

Schedule appointments

There are several ways to **create appointments:**

This is the toolbar button to "Create Appointment."

♦ Click the "Create Appointment" button in the toolbar to get the Appointment dialog box. Enter the information and click OK.

♦ **Or** double-click in a cell to bring up the Appointment dialog box.

♦ **Or** drag across a cell or across several cells. A text field appears in which to type your appointment information.

This is the Appointment dialog box.

Set an alarm to remind you of an appointment. In the Appointment dialog box shown on the opposite page, you see a checkbox labeled "Set Alarm." When you check that box, a field appears in which you can enter how many minutes or hours in advance you'd like to be reminded of the appointment. At that pre-determined time, a reminder dialog box appears on your screen, even if the Palm Desktop Organizer is not open.

This is a handy little reminder. Click the "Snooze" button if you want the reminder to pop up again later.

To edit an appointment in Weekly view

♦ Click once on an existing appointment. A text box appears with an embossed tab on the left side (shown below). Either type in this text box **or** double-click on the embossed tab to open the Appointment dialog box.

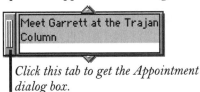

Click this tab to get the Appointment dialog box.

To edit an appointment in Daily or Monthly view

♦ Double-click an appointment to open the Appointment dialog box. Make the edits, then click OK.

♦ In the Daily view (but not the Monthly), you can also use the same technique described above for the Weekly view.

You can **move an appointment** to another time simply by dragging it to another place on the calendar.

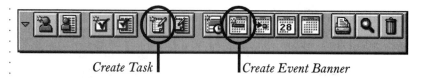

Create Task   *Create Event Banner*

Schedule tasks   In addition to making appointments, you can schedule **Tasks.** Either click the "Create Task" icon in the toolbar (circled above), or double-click a **Task cell** to open the Task dialog box (the **Task cells** are at the bottom of the calendar in the Weekly view, on the right side of the calendar in the Daily view, and appear as bulleted text on the calendar in the Monthly view; see the example on page 36).

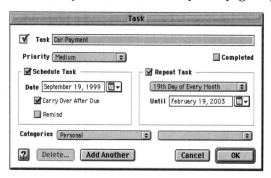

This is the Task dialog box where you can enter the information and the reminder.

While in the Task dialog box, you can set a **reminder** of the task deadline. You can **move** the task to any other day by pressing on the tiny calendar icon (next to the "Date" field) and picking a date from the pull-down menu. If you check the "Repeat Task" checkbox, you'll have lots of choices of how often and when to **repeat** it.

In any calendar view, drag a Task text entry to **move** it to another date.

Create event banners   Besides appointments and tasks, you can create **event banners** that indicate events that span one or more days (up to a year), such as workshops, vacations, or conferences. Click the "Create Event Banner" icon in the toolbar.

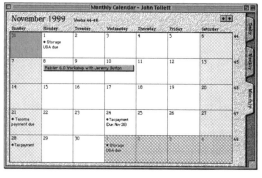

This calendar displays an event banner. Note also that the appearance of the calendar has been modified from plain gray to linen—see the opposite page for details on how to change the appearance.

You can customize the appearance and behavior of your organizer in the **Preferences** dialog box. From the Edit menu, choose "Preferences…."

Customize the appearance

In the Preferences dialog box you can:

♦ Select from fifteen different looks in the "Decor" settings.

♦ Change fonts to any active font on your iBook.

♦ Choose the time increments to show in the calendar time cells (10, 15, 20, or 30 minute increments).

♦ Have your iBook dial telephone numbers in your contact list.

♦ And more.

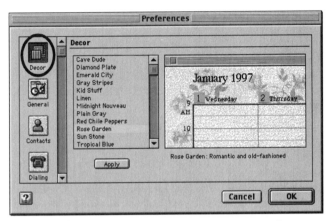

Modify your calendar's appearance and behavior in the Preferences dialog box. Click one of the icons in the left panel, and the options on the right side will change.

Synchronize data with your Palm

If you have a nifty handheld Palm Organizer (shown below), you can automatically synchronize files between the iBook's Palm Desktop Organizer and the handheld device; that is, the data from the Palm can be transferred to the iBook, and the data from the iBook can be transferred to the Palm, all at the same time. If you own a Palm, you'll find all the details about the HotSync operation in your manual and in the online help under the Help menu on your iBook.

The handheld Palm Organizer from 3Com.

For more help

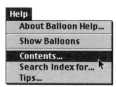

The preceding text will get you started, but for more complete directions and some great tips and shortcuts, press on the Help menu at the top of the screen and pull down to either "Contents...," "Search Index for...," or "Tips...." You can also print up the manuals—look in the Palm Desktop folder for two files called "Getting Started Guide.pdf" and "Palm Desktop Documentation.pdf." Double-click either of them, then print.

Once you get your modem and Internet connection established, you can use the **FAXstf** software that's already installed on your iBook to fax any document that's in your computer. All you do is create your fax message in any software of your choice, then hold down a certain key (explained under Fax Menu; see page 45), and the "Print" menu option turns into "Fax." When you choose "Fax," the FAXstf software opens and you can choose the fax number to send it to. It's great.

FAXstf

When you open the Fax Browser software, it looks like nothing happened! You won't see a dialog box, but you will have the Fax software menu. To get to the Fax Browser itself, go to the Windows menu and choose "Fax Browser," or press Command B.

This is your regular File menu with the options for printing.

When you hold down the hot key, the Print commands change to Fax commands.

And as long as your iBook is turned on, and your modem is plugged in, you can receive faxes in your computer. If you need hard copy of a fax you receive, just print it to your printer. (You do not connect to the Internet to receive a fax!)

Before you send a fax for the first time, open the **Settings** dialog box. You need to enter a few pieces of information for things to work properly.

1. Look in the Applications folder. Find the folder called "FAXstf 5.0."

2. Open the FAXstf folder and double-click the "Fax Browser" icon.

3. From the Edit menu, choose "Settings…" to get the dialog box shown below.

Before you send a fax for the first time

Fax Browser

This is the Fax Browser icon.

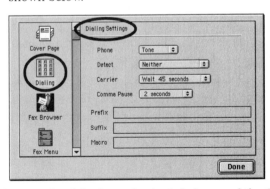

Each icon you click in the left frame will give you different specifications in the right frame.

Click on each of the icons in the left frame of the Settings panel and enter the appropriate information or modify the settings for that item as needed. Most of the items in this panel are self-explanatory. To get started, browse through the following highlights of some of the settings, then consult the manual (also in the FAXstf folder) for details.

Cover Page

Use the **Cover Page Settings** to add your name, company name, voice and fax numbers to a cover page. You can choose to include a cover page with each fax or not, or you can choose to have this information printed at the top of each page. There is actually a law that states you must identify who is sending the fax, so be sure to fill this in properly.

Dialing

The **Dialing Settings** tell your modem how to dial fax numbers.

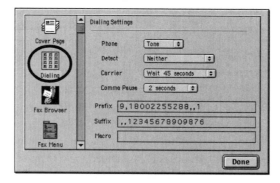

- ◆ **Phone** tells the modem whether your phone is Tone or Pulse (if you have an old, rotary phone, that's definitely pulse).

- ◆ **Detect** determines whether or not the modem waits to detect a dial tone before dialing a number. If you're in a foreign country or have to go through certain switchboards, the modem may not recognize the telephone's dial tone and so it won't dial, so you'd want to set Detect to "Neither" so the modem will be forced to ignore the dial tone and dial the number anyway.

- ◆ **Carrier** sets the length of time the modem waits for a response before hanging up. If you're dialing into a fax machine that is both a fax and answering machine, it may need more time to determine what type of call is coming in.

- ◆ **Comma Pause** sets the time delay assigned to the comma you sometimes need to insert between numbers. These commas are necessary when you need to allow time for outside line access, automated voice instructions, long distance service, or credit card numbers. If the comma(s) you entered into your string of numbers didn't create a pause that was long enough, you can either enter more commas, or change the Comma Pause duration.

  For instance, look at this sequence of numbers:

  9,18002255288,,1

  This would dial 9 for an outside line, wait two seconds for the line to connect, dial the calling card access number, wait four seconds for the automated voice to tell you to press 1 if you want to make a calling card call, then dial that 1.

♦ In the **Prefix** field, enter a number that must be dialed before *every* fax number, such as long distance access codes, credit card numbers, or outside line access on a switchboard system.

♦ In the **Suffix** field, enter a number that must be dialed after *every* fax number, such as the calling card code, a Personal Identification Number (PIN), or maybe a billing number.

Note: Whatever you enter in the Prefix and Suffix fields will dial before and after *every* number. If you travel to different places, check out the Smart Dialing features instead (pages 46–48).

♦ Maybe you use a **phone card** where you type 1) the access number, 2) the PIN number, and *then* 3) the fax number. This is a good time to use the **Macro** field. Type in the entire number, including commas for pauses and the numbers the automated operator asks you to punch. Then when you need to use your phone card, type the letter **M** in front of the fax number.

Different calling cards have different arrangements for the various numbers you have to dial. That is, for some you have to dial the fax number first, then the access code; others you have to dial the access code first then the number, etc. Know your calling card.

Here is an **example** of using a prefix, suffix, and several commas to send a long distance fax from a hotel using a calling card, and a macro to enter an entire phone card number.

The **prefix** forces the modem to dial a 9 for an outside line, wait two seconds, dial the calling card access number, wait four seconds for the automatic operator to ask you to dial 1, then it will dial the 1. After that, the fax number you chose in the main fax browser software kicks in and dials. After that fax number, the **suffix** will cause the modem to wait four seconds while the automated operator tells you to now dial your card number and PIN, and then it will dial those numbers. Whew.

Now, the sequence above is for a calling card that asks for 1) the access code, 2) the number you're calling, and 3) your calling card number and PIN. But a phone card (the kind you buy in a grocery store) usually expects you to dial the fax number *last,* so the card number and PIN are not actually a suffix. So enter your access number and PIN in the "Macro" field, and include pauses for the automatic operator and any numbers she expects you to enter, like "Press 1 if you want English," etc. In your destination fax number, add the letter **M** in front of the fax number.

You might have to experiment to get the correct number of commas in the right places so everything happens at the right time. It helps to call the number with your telephone and listen carefully, making notes as to when and how long you need to pause.

Fax Modem

The **Fax Modem** settings have a couple of important options.

The **Speaker On** menu gives you the option of when, or if, you hear the incredibly irritating sound of the modem connection. It can be useful, though, to hear the modem during those times when you need to troubleshoot the connection. For instance, if you hear a voice through the modem speaker saying, "Who keeps calling this number with their cursed fax machine?" it could be an indication of a wrong fax number.

- ♦ **Never** turns the speaker off.
- ♦ **Always** leaves the speaker on for the entire fax transmission.
- ♦ **During Connect** turns the speaker on only while the modem is connecting.
- ♦ **During Handshake** turns the speaker on while connecting and also between the transmission of pages.

Volume lets you select a sound level for the modem squeal.

Answer On is very important. Here you choose the number of rings the modem waits before answering a call. FAXstf can't tell the difference between a fax call and a voice call, so if you don't have a dedicated fax line and you want to *prevent* your iBook from receiving faxes, choose **Never** from the menu so you can answer the phone. If you find your iBook is not receiving faxes, look in this box and make sure the option does *not* say Never!

The **Send** and **Receive** menus pretend to allow you to set fax transmission rates, although FAXstf will set these speeds automatically depending upon the speed of the modem you're using and the speed of the modem you're calling. Don't be thinkin' that just because you have a 56K modem that you can send faxes at 56K—faxes generally transmit at 14.4 (14,400)!

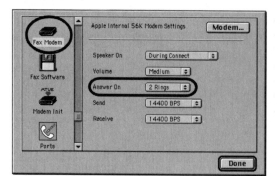

Make sure you choose a certain number of rings to "Answer On" if you want your iBook to automatically pick up faxes sent to you.

The **Fax Software** panel is pretty self-explanatory. The important box to check is **Page Header,** which puts the information from the "Cover Page" settings at the top of each faxed page. Since it's a law that a fax must be identifiable as to where it came from, check this box.

Fax Software

The **Station Message** field can be used to enter an ID number (maximum of 20 characters) that might appear in the display window of the other fax machine (if it has one). Some machines can't read letters in this kind of ID, so don't put anything critical in this field.

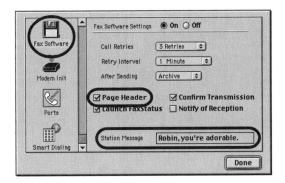

The **Fax Menu** settings allow you to determine which key or combination of keys will be the "activation keys" (hot keys) that change the "Print" menu item to "Fax." For instance, let's say you choose the Command and Option keys in the dialog box shown below, then click "Done." Go to your word processor and type up a memo. Then hold down the Command and Option keys and go to the File menu—you'll see that the usual "Print…" option is now "Fax…" (as shown on page 41) making it an easy shortcut to fax from any open document.

Fax Menu

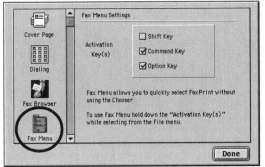

You can choose one, two, or all three keys as your activation shortcut.

Smart Dialing

Smart Dialing is great if you travel to the same places often, such as to a certain hotel or aunt's house or corporate office. You can enter the area code, outside line code, long distance prefix, and long distance suffix for each different place, then save that set of specifications as a "location." When you're ready to fax, choose a location, and all of your calling card numbers and other codes will automatically kick in.

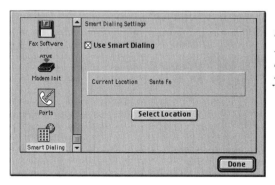

You can choose to enable Smart Dialing or not, depending on what you need to do.

Note: *If you plan to use Smart Dialing, make sure your contact numbers:*

 ♦ *Include the area code.*

 ♦ *Do not include the long distance prefix of 1.*

♦ Smart Dialing does not work with international numbers.

♦ If Smart Dialing is enabled, the prefix and suffix numbers you entered in the Dialing Settings (page 42) are disabled.

♦ The Macro number you may have set in Dialing Settings (pages 42 and 43) can be used in locations.

To set up a new location

1. Click the "Select Location" button. You'll get a Location List, shown below, left.

2. Double-click one of the empty fields in the Location List. The Edit Location window opens, shown below, right.

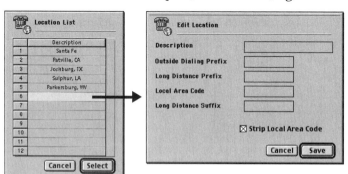

3. In the **Description** field, type a name that describes the location, such as "Uncle Cliff's House" or "Ritz, San Francisco."

4. In the **Outside Dialing Prefix,** type the number for an outside line, if necessary, and if you plan to use a calling card, type the access code here also, including commas (see page 43 for details about how to enter your calling card number properly).

   ♦ So if you're at Uncle Cliff's house and you *won't* be using a calling card, this field would be blank.

   ♦ If you're at Uncle Cliff's house and *will* be using a calling card, enter the card access number (the 1-800 number; see page 43).

   ♦ If you're at your corporate office and you need to dial 9 to get an outside line (but don't need a calling card), enter 9.

   ♦ If you're in a hotel and need to use a calling card, enter 9 (or whatever the outside line number is), and the commas and calling card access numbers necessary.

5. In the **Long Distance Prefix,** enter the number you need to dial before the area code and fax number, if any. In most of the States, this would be the number 1. Enter it even if all the fax calls you plan to make are not long distance—the software will decide whether to use the number or not.

   Now, if you plan to use a Smart Dialing location, this means you should not enter the 1 directly into the fax number in the contact list!

6. The **Local Area Code** refers to the area code of the location where you will be dialing from. For instance, if the location is Uncle Cliff's house, enter the area code where Uncle Cliff lives.

7. The **Long Distance Suffix** is where you enter your calling card number and PIN, if you're using a calling card. Again, see page 43 for details on this. If you're not using a calling card, credit card, and your corporate office doesn't require any sort of billing account code or something, this would be blank.

8. Check the box to **Strip Local Area Code.** The software will check to see if the local area code you entered in this panel is the same as the one you're calling and will automatically remove it.

   This means, however, that you must enter the area code in every fax number in your contact list!

See the following page for some examples of locations.

To keep your entire contact system consistent, *it's a good idea to make yourself a home base location, even if you don't think you'll need another location for a while. Then in your Phonebook list, always include the area code, and leave off the long distance prefix of (usually) 1.*

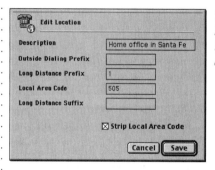

This is a typical location from a home office where you don't need to dial an outside line or use a credit card or calling card.

This is a typical location from a hotel where you need to dial an outside line and use a calling card. Even though you can't see all the numbers in the Prefix and Suffix fields, they're there.

If you created a Macro number (page 43), you can just enter the letter "M" in the appropriate space.

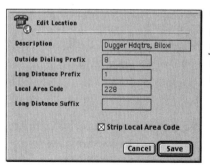

This is a typical location from corporate headquarters where you do need to dial an outside line, but they don't expect you to use a calling card.

To choose a location

1. When you want to choose or change locations, open the Fax Browser software.

2. From the Edit menu, choose "Settings...."

3. Scroll down and click once on "Smart Dialing."

4. If "Smart Dialing" is unchecked, check it.

5. Click the "Select Location" button.

6. Click once on the desired location, then click the "Select" button. Put the Settings box away (click the "Done" button).

7. Proceed to send your fax.

Now add your list of fax numbers to the Phonebook. Open the Fax Browser software. Then:

Add fax numbers to the Phonebook

1. From the Windows menu, choose "Fax Numbers."

   Or if you already have the browser window open, press the Phonebook button (![icon]). You'll see this window:

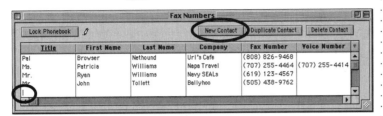

2. Click the "New Contact" button. This unlocks the Phonebook (notice the button in the upper-left corner) and puts a cursor in the blank line, ready for you to enter information. Press the Tab key to move the cursor from one column to the next.

   As soon as you enter a "Title," it will automatically alphabetize itself into the correct row. You don't have to type the parentheses around the area code—just type the ten-digit number, and when you hit Tab or click anywhere, the formatting will be automatically applied.

We're assuming you have looked through the previous eight pages and entered the appropriate settings before you try to send your first fax. If you haven't done that yet, please do so.

Send that fax!

There are lots more little tricks this software does, but you've got a great manual in the FAXstf folder. Just double-click it and print it up.

To send a fax, you don't really need to open the fax software (unless you want to send a QuickNote; choose it from the File menu in the Fax Browser software). Create your document in any software you choose. Then, right there with that document on your screen:

1. Hold down the activation key(s) you selected (page 45), then from the File menu, choose "Fax…."

2. The FaxPrint dialog box will open. Drag the name of the fax recipient from the left window and drop it in the Destinations window on the right. If you don't have the address you want in the Phonebook yet, press on the "Fax Numbers" menu and choose "Temporary Address…" to enter a number.

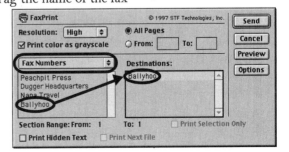

3. Click the "Send" button.

AppleCD Audio Player

You can play any of your audio CDs on your iBook. The quality of the sound might not be great, but you can add speakers if you find you use your iBook as a CD player regularly.

To play an audio CD

1. Open the sliding CD drawer on the right side of the iBook by pushing the round-cornered rectangular button.

2. Put an audio CD in the tray, press down firmly on the spool, and push the drawer shut. The CD icon will appear on the Desktop and start playing automatically.

To make the CD Player visible on the Desktop

♦ Go to the Apple menu and choose "AppleCD Audio Player." This gives you a full audio console to control the playing of the CD, as shown below.

The console has most of the features of a real CD player, plus a few extras. Try these:

The clock

♦ Press on the tiny clock in the upper-left of the player and choose whether to display the elapsed or remaining time of the entire disc or of each individual track.

The control buttons

Use the control buttons as you would in a regular player.

♦ The **Normal** button is the default setting that plays the tracks in the same order as they appear on the CD.

♦ The **Shuffle** button randomly shuffles the tracks into a different order every time you click it.

♦ Click the **Prog** (Program) button, then click the tiny arrow you see under the "Normal" button to see a track list. Now you can manually rearrange the tracks in any order you want. Just drag a track from the left panel (Tracks) to the right panel (PlayList); drag the songs in the order you want them listed in the play list.

To remove a track from the PlayList, simply drag it out of the right panel and drop it onto the Desktop; it will disappear.

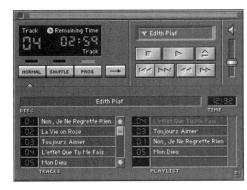

Drag the name of a song from the Tracks side and drop it on the PlayList side to rearrange the order of the songs.

♦ The **Arrow** button indicates that the CD will play to its end and stop. You can instruct the player to loop (continuously replay) the CD: click the Arrow button and it changes to a **Loop** button, causing the CD to continue playing until you pause or stop it.   *Loop button*

To expand the player to see a complete list of audio tracks and to rename the tracks, click the "Normal" button, then click the small triangle just below "Normal." You'll see this:

Rename the tracks

If you like an organized feeling, type in the name of the CD in the "Disc" field. Then single-click in each "PlayList" field and type to replace the generic track names with actual song names. This is entirely optional, but it enables you to easily select favorite tracks. (These custom entries won't appear if you play the CD on another computer.)

To **manually select** a specific track to play, double-click on the audio track number in the far-left column.

The buttons . The **buttons** on the AppleCD Audio Player act very similarly to the ones on your real CD player.

 Click the **Stop** button to stop a CD from playing. Now, when you click Play (the middle button), the CD will start playing the first track in the PlayList.

 The **Play** button starts the music. As soon as you click it, the button becomes the **Pause** button.

 Pause pauses the CD, and when you click this button again, the song resumes playing where it was stopped.

 The **Eject** button ejects the CD. (You can also eject a CD while you're at the Desktop: select the CD icon, then press Command E.)

 Click once on the **Back** button to return to the start of the current audio track. *Hold down* the Back button to cycle backward through the tracks.

 Click once on the **Forward** button to move to the next track in the PlayList. *Hold down* the Forward button to cycle forward through the audio tracks.

 Hold down the **Fast Rewind** button to move backward quickly through the current audio track.

 Hold down the **Fast Forward** button to move forward quickly through the current audio track.

 The **Speaker Volume** slider adjusts the sound level.

Keyboard shortcuts · Here are a couple of nifty **keyboard shortcuts**. Use the arrow keys you
for buttons · see on the lower-right side of your keyboard.

♦ Adjust the volume with the UpArrow and DownArrow keys.

♦ Return to the beginning of a song by tapping the LeftArrow key.

♦ Cycle forward through tracks by tapping the RightArrow key.

If the CD player console is collapsed (small, as shown below) instead of expanded, you still have **access to the PlayList:** click on the small triangle in the upper-right of the window, which opens a menu of the PlayList (shown below). The CD title that appears in this window is "Audio CD" unless you previously typed a name in the "Disc" field of the expanded player, as described on page 51.

Access the PlayList

Press on this tiny arrow to get the menu of song titles.

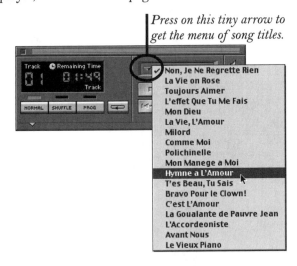

To economize Desktop space, double-click the embossed title bar (even though there's no title in it) at the top of the player and the panel will collapse to show only the bar with the Close box. Double-click the bar again whenever you need access to the controls.

Roll up the window

This is the title bar of the CD player. Double-click it to display the console again.

(If the double-click doesn't "roll up" the window to just the bar, you might need to turn on the "windowshade" feature. From the Apple menu, get the "Appearance" control panel. Click the "Options" tab. Make sure there is a check in the checkbox labeled "Double-click title bar to collapse windows." Close the control panel.)

Get the AppleCD Audio Player Guide from the **Help** menu. Click on a topic or phrase, then click OK.

For more help

Netscape Communicator

See Chapter 6 for information about using Netscape for email.

Netscape Communicator is a software program, called a browser, that enables you to see web pages on the World Wide Web, after you have first set up your Internet connection with an ISP (Internet service provider). There are so many more tips and tricks than we have room for here, so poke around in the menus and especially in the Preferences (from the Edit menu).

Type in a web address here, then click Return to go to that page. You don't have to type **http://**.

Type words for stuff you want to find, such as "Robert Burns," then hit Return. Try it!

The pointer turns into the browser hand whenever it is positioned over a link. Click once to jump to the linked page.

When you find a page you like a lot, make a bookmark of it, as described on page 56. But for extra-special pages, put a bookmark right in the toolbar: Go to the page you love, then drag this little bookmark icon down to the toolbar directly below and drop it. Edit the toolbar bookmarks like any other bookmarks; see page 57.

File Edit View Go Bookmarks Communicator Help   2:27 PM

Netscape: Url's Internet Cafe. E-mail Tips

Back Forward Reload Home Search Netscape Images Print Security Stop   N

Location: http://www.urlsinternetcafe.com/junkmail   What's Related

Robin Williams   Url's Internet   Panorama Point   Amazon.com   Lucas   BookWire

Index   Coffee Bar   Gift Shop   Classroom   Basement   Cafe Staff   Contact Us   Attic

Url's Internet Cafe

Classroom

Back to the Classroom

eMail tips: Junk eMail

Url demonstrates his method of reading junk eMail.

Url's take on (well-intentioned) junk eMail.

A lot of people are buying computers for the first time. They're using eMail for the first time. And they're sending junk mail for the first time. This is actually an interesting phenomenon, because these people

The lock icon indicates a secure page as opposed to a non-secure page. If you are sending important information like a credit card number, this icon should be in the locked position.

The little connection icon indicates if you are actually online or not. If you're not, these connectors are separated.

These buttons open other parts of the Netscape Communicator package. Click on the far left end of this mini toolbar to open the floating palette, shown below.

Navigator *is the browser you're using right now.*

Inbox *opens the email program, discussed in Chapter 6.*

Newsgroups *opens the newsreader if you have arranged with your service provider to receive newsgroup postings.*

Address Book *opens the address book for your email, which is only handy if you use Netscape as your email program.*

Composer *is a program in which you can create your own web pages.*

Click the edges of these various toolbars and they will roll up so you have more room on the screen.

You can also rearrange the toolbars, if you like— just drag their left edges.

*If your toolbars are gone, how will you go back and forward through the pages? Just **hold** the mouse button down in any blank spot on the screen, and a menu pops up where you can choose Back or Forward, as shown.*

You can also use the Go menu or the keyboard shortcuts— Command] to go back, and Command [to go forward.

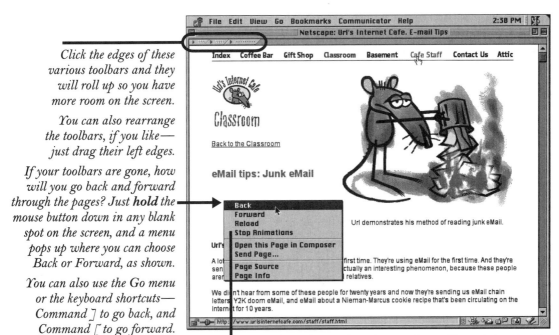

Notice in this menu there is an option to "Stop Animations." While the page is loading, this option says "Stop Loading." After the page has loaded, if there are continuous animations on the page (in this example, Url's fire is burning), the option changes to "Stop Animations." It's the same in the View menu.

Check this "What's Related" button regularly. On many sites, such as the screenwriting site I was viewing, this button offers a lot of great info, and you can even add to the information to make it more useful for others (choose "Suggest related sites…").

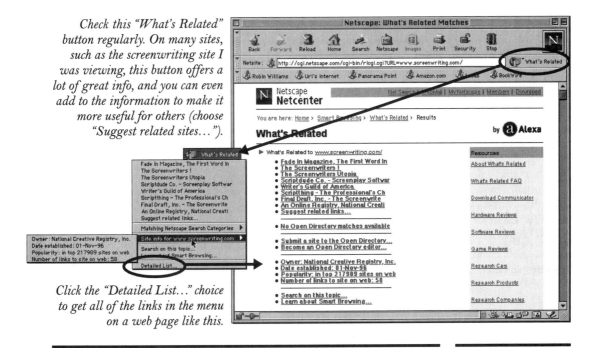

Click the "Detailed List…" choice to get all of the links in the menu on a web page like this.

Bookmark your favorite pages

It's inevitable that you'll find web pages you'll want to return to. Just like you would put bookmarks in a book, you can put bookmarks on web pages so you can click back to them instantly. Here are a few tips for using Netscape bookmarks.

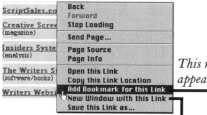

♦ **To make a bookmark,** go to the page you like and press Command D, or choose "Add Bookmark" from the Bookmarks menu. The new bookmark will instantly appear at the bottom of the Bookmarks menu, shown to the left.

♦ You can make a bookmark **without actually going to the page.** You might find a page with lots of links, many of which you want to bookmark. So instead of *clicking* on the link, *press* the mouse button down and hold it down—a menu will pop up (shown below). Choose "Add Bookmark for this Link."

This new bookmark will appear in the menu.

*Notice you can also choose **"New Window with this Link."** This is great—open a new window, then you'll always have the original page full of links to go back to (use the Communicator menu to choose different open pages).*

♦ **Organize your bookmarks** into individual folders: From the Bookmarks menu, choose "Edit Bookmarks." You'll get the window shown below. Go to the File menu and choose "New Folder…," name it, and then you can drag bookmarks into it.

♦ To **delete** a bookmark, select it, then hit the Delete key.

*If you're working on a project and you want **all of the bookmarks you make to go into one folder,** do this: Click once on the folder in this window. From the View menu, choose "Set as New Bookmarks Folder." The chosen folder gets a little ribbon on it, as shown, circled.*

*The **question mark** means you haven't actually been to that page yet.*

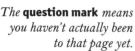

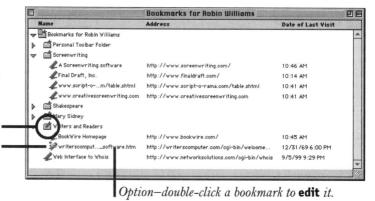

*Option–double-click a bookmark to **edit** it.*

As noted at the bottom of the previous page, you can hold down the Option key and double-click on any bookmark to **edit** it. You'll get the dialog box shown below where you can change the name, update the link, add comments, etc. This is great—notice the difference in the unedited and edited bookmark menus below.

Edit the bookmarks

There are lots more book-mark tips. Poke around and discover things. Also check the tips at **www.UrlsInternetCafe.com/ classroom**.

Edit your bookmarks into names that make sense to you.

Change this awkward collection of bookmarks into . . .

. . . this nice, neat package.

We guarantee most web pages will be so much easier to read if you change your **default fonts** to New York and Monaco. Try it and see.

Change your default fonts

1. From the Edit menu, choose "Preferences…."

2. In the left panel, choose "Fonts."

3. In the right panel, press on the menu for "Variable Width Font" and choose New York. Make sure the "Size" is 12.

4. Press on the menu for "Fixed Width Font" and choose Monaco. Change the "Size" to 12.

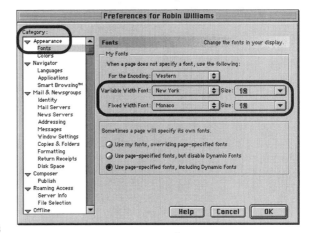

Don't be intimidated by the Preferences! Get in there and see what makes sense. Change the obvious things, and just ignore what you don't know.

Microsoft Internet Explorer

Internet Explorer is a software program, called a browser, that enables you to see web pages on the World Wide Web *after* you have first set up your Internet connection with an ISP (Internet service provider). Yes, you have two browsers on your iBook (this one and Netscape Communicator). Play around with both and see which one suits you better.

Use the choices in the Favorites menu to create, organize, and edit your bookmarks (called Favorites).

Click these buttons to make the type on the page larger or smaller.

If you click the Mail icon, the program Outlook Express will open. Explorer does not have its own mail client.

Put Favorites in the toolbar: go to the page you want, then from the Favorites menu, choose "Add Page to Toolbar Favorites."

Delete or edit the Toolbar Favorites in the "Favorites" window; see opposite page.

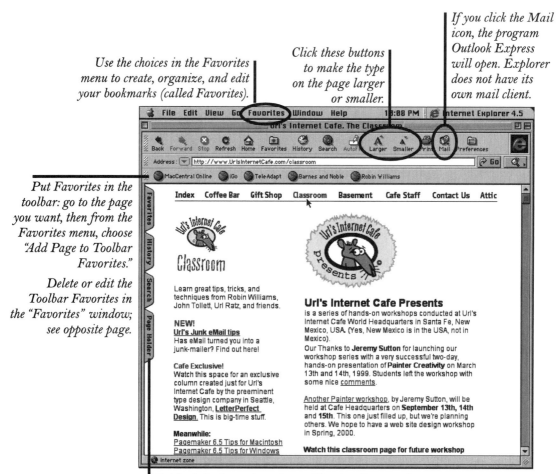

Robin finds these tabs to be terribly visually annoying.

Click the Favorites tab to get a really obnoxious panel that displays your Favorites and covers up half the web page.

Click the History tab to change the panel to a list of all the pages you've been to for the past month (details on page 60).

Click the Search tab for access to selected search tools.

See the opposite page for information about the Page Holder.

To put the panels back, click on the same tab you clicked to open it.

Favorites are a way to keep track of your favorite sites and return to them with the click of a button. If you're accustomed to bookmarks in Netscape, you'll find Favorites now work very much the same way in Internet Explorer. Of course.

♦ Go to a web page you like, then press Command D, or choose "Add Page to Favorites" from the Favorites menu.

♦ Like the Netscape example on page 56, you can press on a link and make a favorite to it without having to go there first.

♦ To edit, delete, and organize favorites, press Command J, or choose "Organize Favorites" from the Favorites menu. Use the Favorites menu to add new folders to the Favorites window. Drag Favorites into folders, drag folders and Favorites around to organize them, and edit them as you would any file name.

Favorites

Use this menu to add and organize your Favorites.

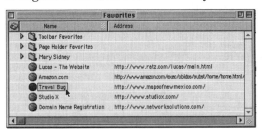

You can edit your Toolbar Favorites here, also. You might want to shorten their names so you can fit more in the toolbar.

The **Page Holder** panel is an interesting concept. If you come across a page with lots of links that you want to keep track of, you can put the page in the Page Holder: Click on the Page Holder tab, then click the tiny icon in the upper-right of the panel. If you want to see just the links and eliminate all the graphics, click the link button.

Page Holder

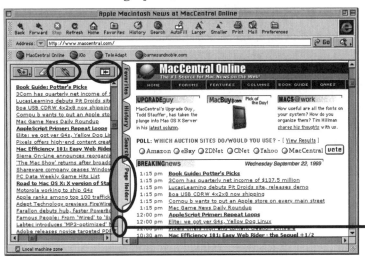

To resize the panel, *press on this divider and drag left or right.*

History Internet Explorer keeps track of every page you've been to for quite a while. To see the list of those pages, click the History tab, shown below. Each day's pages are in a folder; click the triangle next to the folder to get to the pages inside. Internet Explorer not only keeps a list of the pages you've been to in this browser, but if you (or anyone else in your home or office) uses America Online to cruise around the web, every one of *those* pages will also show up in this list.

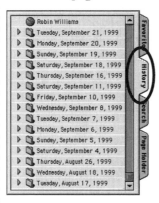

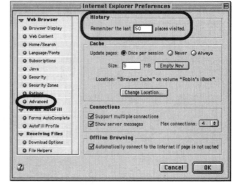

This is the History list.   *The number of pages listed in History is set in Preferences (from the Edit menu) in the Advanced section. The default is 300 pages.*

Now, all of us at one time or another have popped into a web page or two that we really don't want to brag about.

You can give the History.html file to someone else to enjoy. To open it, drag the file icon and drop it on top of a browser icon, or drop it right in the middle of any open web page.

To delete any or all pages from the History list

1. From the Go menu, choose "Open History."

2. Click on the web page you want to delete, or hold down the Shift key and click on several pages you want to delete, or press Command A to select all.

3. From the Edit menu, choose "Clear." Close the window.

You can **export the History list** as a web page, then open that page and each of the sites you've visited will be an actual link (as shown to the left). Once you've exported the links, you can delete them from the History list and you'll still have every one in the exported file.

1. From the go menu, choose "Open History."

2. From the File menu, choose "Export…."

3. Keep the name History.html and save the file.

4. To open the file, go to the File menu and choose "Open File…." Find "History.html" and click Open.

The best way to learn how to use **America Online** (affectionately called AOL) and all the features it offers is to poke around. Check out everything in the menus and everything in the toolbar across the top.

America Online

Use the menus and the toolbar to discover everything about AOL. Don't forget the Help menu! You can use that when you're offline. For more detailed help information, choose "Member Services Online Help" from the Help menu when you're connected. You can even write to the AOL guides and ask specific questions.

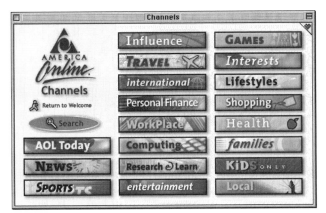

*See Chapter 6 for tips on how to use **AOL email**.*

Right beneath the Welcome screen when you first log on is this Channels window. Click any button to go to that area.

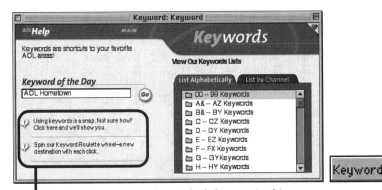

Use the Keyword window to look for certain things: press Command K to bring it up, or click the "Keyword" button in the browser toolbar, right below the Weather button. If you don't know what to look for, click either of the buttons on the left side (circled, above) to either learn more about Keywords or to choose one at random. Try it!

To the Internet • To get to the **Internet** and the World Wide Web through America Online, either type in a web address in the location box and hit Return, or go to the Internet menu in the toolbar and choose "Go to the Web" to open the browser that AOL uses.

The Back and Forward buttons are way over here.

You can use Netscape as your browser • AOL uses a version of Microsoft Internet Explorer as its browser. If you prefer **Netscape,** use it: Log in to AOL, then double-click your Netscape icon. There you are, cruising the web in Netscape while on your AOL connection.

Favorites • That little heart you see in the corners of pages can be used to make **Favorites** of web pages. While you're viewing a page you like, click on the little heart. You'll get a message asking, among other things, if you want to add it to your Favorite Places. Click "Yes."

Favorites will be listed in the Favorites menu in the toolbar.

To **edit, delete, or organize them,** go to the Favorites menu and choose "Favorite Places." You get this window where you can move the favorites around, delete them, rename them, and so on.

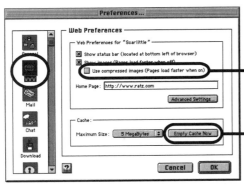

If the graphics on the web pages look awful, uncheck this box.

If AOL seems to be moving very slowly, click this button.

Extra tips in AOL
Check out the Preferences (under the "My AOL" menu) for lots of customizing options. If you don't know what something is, leave it alone!

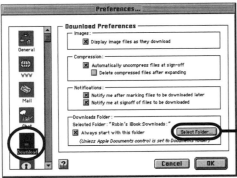

To prevent large files from automatically downloading to your computer before you have a chance to see who they're from (and so have a chance to delete them before they download), uncheck this box.

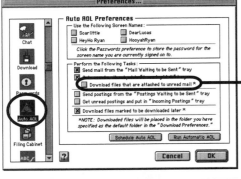

So you can find files that are downloaded, create a folder on your hard disk called "Downloads." Then come to this preference and tell AOL to use that folder.

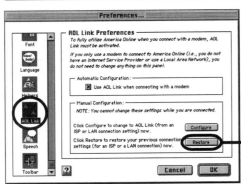

If you use an Internet service provider or if you're on a network, like in a large office, this AOL Link thing will make you crazy (if you haven't run into the problem, don't read the rest of this). You can switch back to your ISP connection here, or, better yet, go to Setup at the Welcome screen and choose the billing option to BYOA (Bring Your Own Access) so you can use your own ISP to log onto AOL. It's cheaper (about $10/month) and you avoid having to turn the AOL Link on and off.

**EarthLink
Total Access**

EarthLink is a *national* Internet servicer provider, which means they have local phone numbers all over the country for connecting. If you use Apple's Internet Setup Assistant (explained in Chapter 4), you can establish your connection with EarthLink right on your iBook. (Your other option is to find a local service provider in your town.)

An advantage for travelers is that as an EarthLink subscriber you can get local phone numbers to the Internet in most other American towns and cities, as well as overseas. Watch the fine print—connecting from Hawaii and Alaska is the same (to EarthLink) as making an international connection and costs an extra $9 an hour (this may change as their merger with MindSpring, a huge international provider, evolves).

If you connect to EarthLink through the iBook, the first 30 days are free, and the $25 setup fee is waived. After that, it's $19.95 a month for unlimited access (that means you can be on as long as you want, any time of the day or night). They offer other services, like special deals for travelers. Check around the web site when you get there.

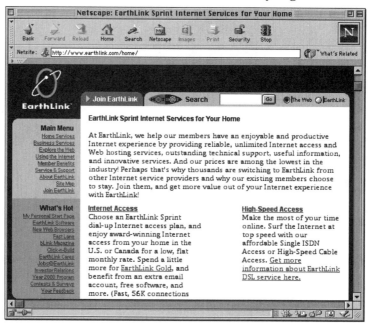

If you use AOL, **you don't need EarthLink.** If you decide not to use EarthLink, toss the folder called "EarthLink Total Access" because it takes almost 63 megabytes of hard disk space. To find that folder, open the "Internet" folder, then open the "Internet Access" folder.

**Microsoft
Outlook Express**

See Chapter 6 for information about using Outlook Express for email.

Need a break from all the productivity the iBook is providing you? Become Rollie McFly, the only remaining Rollie Pollie in the **Bugdom** that has a chance of rescuing all the Lady Bugs who've been captured and held prisoner by the evil Fire Ants. You must fight your way to the Ant Hill, if you can find it, and have a final showdown with King Thorax, leader of the Fire Ants. If you're successful, you'll be the new ruler of the Bugdom as peace and harmony return.

Be sure to read the PDF manual in the Bugdom folder for complete instructions. If you're playing Bugdom while in a client meeting or in the classroom, don't forget to mute the speaker *before* you start the game. Once the game has started, the mute button (F6) won't work.

After you've started Bugdom, you can speed past the first several introductory pages by clicking on them.

Bugdom

This game takes up 67 megabytes of your hard disk space, so if you never play it, toss it.

EdView is password-protected software that limits Internet access to millions of teacher-approved web pages, assuring you that your children are not exposed to sites that are inappropriate. After you've installed EdView from the CD and entered a password, a feature called "Channel Lock" limits web access to sites that are in the EdView database. EdView installs an "EV" menu item and icon on the right side of the Desktop menu bar that enables you to turn EdView on or off. You can "Disable Channel Lock" by choosing that option from the "EV" pull-down menu—enter your password in the "Login" window that appears and your web access is unlimited. Whenever necessary you can return to the "EV" menu and choose "Enable Channel Lock."

EdView Internet Safety Kit

Make any web site accessible by entering its address into the "Sites" section of the "Preferences" dialog box: From the "EV" menu, choose "Edit Preferences…," enter your password in the "Login" window, and click OK. Then click the "Sites" tab in the Preferences dialog box to add web site addresses you want to be accessible.

If a child tries to access a web site that's not in the EdView database or that hasn't been manually entered in the "Sites" list, this is the page that appears in the browser:

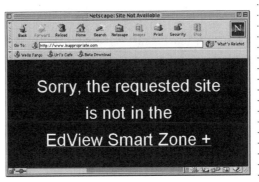

QuickTime

QuickTime is Apple's amazing, industry-standard software for creating and playing video, sound, music, pictures, interactive images, and 3D graphics. Most of the time you'll enjoy a QuickTime-enhanced computer experience without being aware that QuickTime even exists. In fact, you really don't need to worry about it—*you* won't actually *use* QuickTime; your computer uses it to make things happen for you.

PictureViewer

QuickTime PictureViewer opens many types of image files. To view an image file, drag it on top of the QuickTime PictureViewer icon. This little utility is so great for viewing images that we suggest you make an alias of the viewer and leave it on your Desktop. Whenever you get an image file, drag it on top of the PictureViewer for an instant presentation of the image.

PictureViewer

Make an alias for the Desktop so you can drop image files on it for viewing.

To make an alias of the QuickTime PictureViewer

1. Open the QuickTime folder, found in the Applications folder.
2. Hold down the Command and Option keys.
3. While those keys are held down, drag the QuickTime PictureViewer icon to the Desktop. This will make an alias on the Desktop, as shown to the right.

QuickTime Player

QuickTime Player plays multimedia files. Drag a QuickTime movie or animated GIF file and drop it on top of the QuickTime Player to play the file. You already have an alias of this player on your Desktop so you can easily play any movie you find.

QuickTime Updater

The **QuickTime Updater** is an easy way to keep your copy of QuickTime updated to the most current, latest, and greatest version. Double-click the Updater icon and the iBook will connect to the QuickTime web site and check to see if there's a newer version of QuickTime available. If there is, the Updater will automatically download any files necessary to your iBook and update the QuickTime software.

QuickTime Plugin

The **QuickTime Plugin** is already installed in the Plugin folders of three applications that came bundled with your iBook: Internet Explorer, Netscape Communicator, and America Online. This plugin enables you to view, hear, and interact with QuickTime-enhanced web pages.

You might have these icons on your Desktop, shown to the right. This is what they do. If you don't ever use these, feel free to toss them.

The **Mac OS Info Center** is a web site that is not really on the web—it's on your hard disk, so when you double-click this icon it opens a browser and finds the web pages but does not connect to the Internet (unless you click an "outside" link). Any text that is blue and underlined is a link; click on a link to jump to another page with more information. Just be careful to take note of the links that actually lead to the Internet—don't click them until you have set up a connection with an Internet service provider. If you use America Online, log on to AOL first, then go to the Desktop and double-click "Mac OS Info Center."

Mac OS Info Center

If you double-click **Browse the Internet,** your iBook will try to connect to the Internet and open a browser. Don't click this until you have first set up your Internet connection! If, after you're set up, you find you don't use this icon because you usually connect from a menu item or by double-clicking something else, you can toss this icon in the garbage (it's just a "script," a small piece of programming). If you do like to use it, you can change the default browser that it opens: go to the Internet control panel (page 88), click the "Web" tab, and change the "Default Web Browser."

Browse the Internet

The **Mail** icon represents a script that opens your email program for you. Its default is to open Microsoft Outlook Express, but you can change that if you have a different email program that you prefer. Change the default through the Internet control panel, under the "E-Mail" tab (see page 87).

Mail

Toss the Mail icon if you don't think you'll ever use it. You will still be able to open your email program without it.

This **QuickTime Player** icon on your Desktop is an alias to the original program, as mentioned on the opposite page. Drag any little movie file you might have onto this icon, drop it, and the QuickTime Player will open and load the movie. When the player opens, click the big, round button to play the movie. You'll find a sample movie in the QuickTime folder, which is inside the Applications folder.

QuickTime Player

Fonts

All of the fonts installed with Mac OS 8.6 are TrueType fonts (as opposed to PostScript Type 1 fonts). This means the fonts will print fine to an inexpensive printer, but are not appropriate for professional design work that will be output on an expensive, high-end imagesetter.

*A number of these fonts are specially created to be used cross-platform; that is, if you use them in your documents, a PC (using something like Windows 95 or 98) will read the same font just fine. Conversely, if a Windows user uses these cross-platform fonts, the fonts should display on your iBook (or on any Mac) just fine. The trick is to use the keyboard shortcut or the menu shortcut to make the face italic or bold; that is, don't choose the actual "Times New Roman Italic" typeface from the menu, as you may be accustomed to doing for professional work.

If you want to understand everything about fonts on your Macintosh, read How to Boss Your Fonts Around, *second edition, by Robin.*

The following fonts (typefaces) are installed on your iBook. If you don't see an italic or bold version below, that means the font doesn't really include an italic or bold version. You can use your keyboard or menu commands to *make* a face italic or bold, but it probably won't look very good when printed. If you print to a PostScript printer, the fake italic or bold will be stripped away and the face will print in the regular style.

*Arial	New York
*Arial Black	Palatino
CAPITALS	*Palatino Italic*
Charcoal	**Palatino Bold**
Chicago	***Palatino Bold Italic***
*Comic Sans	Sand
Courier	Symbol: Σψμβολ
Courier Bold	**Techno**
*Courier New	*Textile*
*Courier New Italic	Times
	Times Italic
*Courier New Bold	**Times Bold**
*Courier New Bold Italic	***Times Bold Italic***
	*Times New Roman
Gadget	**Times New Roman Italic*
Geneva	***Times New Roman Bold**
Georgia	****Times New Roman Bold Italic***
Georgia Italic	Trebuchet
Georgia Bold	*Trebuchet Italic*
Georgia Bold Italic	**Trebuchet Bold**
Helvetica	***Trebuchet Bold Italic***
Helvetica Bold	*Verdana
*Impact	**Verdana Italic*
Minion Web	***Verdana Bold**
Monaco	****Verdana Bold Italic***
Monotype.com	*Webdings: ▶ 📖 ⚓ 🕷 ⓘ 📨 ✂ 📷 ♥

The Keyboard

Although you are probably used to the keyboard on a computer, the iBook keyboard has some special features. For instance, even though you don't see a **numeric keypad,** there actually is one embedded.

Some of the **Fkeys** across the top of the keyboard (F1–F12) can fulfill more than one function, and some can be programmed for extra features.

The **modifier keys** are the keys that don't do anything all by themselves: Shift, Command (the one with the apple symbol), Control (ctrl), Option (option or alt), and Function (fn). Although the Enter key technically isn't a modifier key because when you press it you see something happen, we're going to include it in this group because on the iBook keyboard the Enter key can change its function.

The **arrow keys** also turn into the Page Up, Page Down, Home, and End keys that you may be used to from using a standard keyboard.

You can change the functions of the keys using the **fn** (Function) key, **num lock,** and the **Keyboard Control Panel,** as explained in the rest of this chapter.

Fkeys

The **Fkeys** (function keys) are the keys across the top of the keyboard labeled F1 through F12. On every Mac keyboard, Apple has programmed F1 through F4 as keyboard shortcuts:

F1	Undo
F2	Cut
F3	Copy
F4	Paste

The other Fkeys have traditionally been left available for you to assign as hot keys in your various applications. For instance, the screen capture software we use to make the screen shots in this book (Captivate Select) let us assign an Fkey to take the shot. On the iBook, Apple has programmed extra features into a number of the Fkeys, as noted below, plus you can assign features to other keys.

The Function Key (fn)

This is what will happen if the checkbox in the "Hot Function Keys" window is checked; see page 74.

If you hold down the **fn** key (bottom-left of the keyboard), the action of keys F1 through F6 change from their usual roles to **Control Buttons.** Control Buttons adjust the screen brightness, speaker volume, speaker muting, and set the num lock (numbers lock; see page 73).

When the Fkeys are in Control Button mode, this is what they do:

F1	decreases the screen's brightnesss
F2	increases the screen's brightness
F3	decreases the built-in speaker volume
F4	increases the built-in speaker volume
F5	turns on the num lock feature (see page 73)
F6	mutes the built-in speaker

User-Definable Fkeys

Fkeys F7 through F12 are **user-definable.** That is, you can program them yourself to open often-used applications or documents, evoke an AppleScript, or log on to a file server. You can even program a key to go directly to your favorite web site.

The first time you press one of these function keys, you'll get a "Hot Function Keys" window on your screen (shown on the opposite page).

♦ Select an application, document, AppleScript, or volume on a network that you want to launch whenever you hit the selected Fkey.

♦ Or drag any icon from your Desktop into this dialog box and drop it into one of the Fkey slots. Then when you hit that Fkey, the application or document represented by that icon will open.

The variety of stickers that came with your iBook can be applied to your keyboard to remind you of each key's newly assigned function.

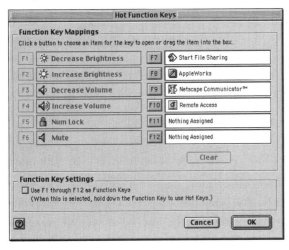

This is the Hot Function Keys dialog box where you can customize the actions of several of the Fkeys. See page 74 for more details.

Below is an illustration showing the regular keys in grey and the Fkeys and modifier keys in white. Press the **fn** key down (circled, below left) to change the functions of the various keys, as indicated. See the following page for details about the modifier and arrow keys.

The Keyboard Illustrated

The illustrations to the left show what will happen if the checkbox in the "Hot Function Keys" window is checked; see page 74.

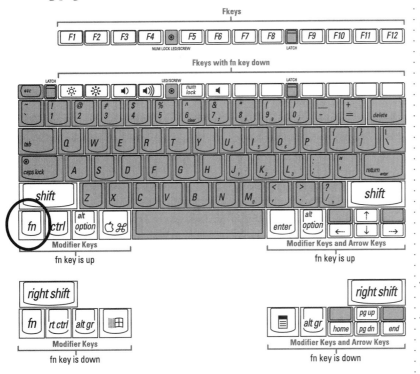

Notice you get several extra "Right Shift" keys, plus a Right Control key. These are useful in games or other software where the right-side keys can have different features from the left-side keys.

We haven't been able to find anyone who can tell us what the "alt gr" keys are for. If you find out, please let us know.

Modifier Keys

As shown on the previous page, holding down the **fn** key also affects certain **modifier keys.**

The **arrow keys** on the bottom-right of the keyboard that usually move the text cursor become page navigation keys when you hold down the **fn** key: Home, Page Up, Page Down, and End. Some applications use these keys as shortcuts, not just on your iBook, but on any Mac. For instance, PageMaker uses Page Up and Page Down to turn pages; Netscape uses Page Up and Page Down to pop to the top or bottom of a web page; Microsoft Word uses Home and End to pop to the top or bottom of the page that's visible on your screen (and if you hold down the Shift key in Word and press Home or End, the text from the cursor to the top or bottom of the page becomes selected).

The **Control key,** when you hold down the **fn** key, becomes the Right Control key, and the **Shift key** becomes the Right Shift key. The **Option keys** become Alt GR keys, and we haven't been able to find anyone who knows what these are.

This is the icon for the Windows key.

This is the icon for the Windows Menu key.

The **Option, Command,** and **Enter keys** take on the functions of certain keys on a PC keyboard when you hold down the **fn** key. This is useful if you're running Windows emulation software, such as Insignia Soft-Windows or Connectix Virtual PC, that lets your Mac use Windows software. As shown on the previous page, the Command key becomes the **Windows key** that brings up the Windows Start menu. The Enter key becomes the **Windows Menu key** that accesses the right-button menus (like the Mac's contextual menus). And the Option key becomes an official **Windows Alt key.**

If you look carefully at your iBook keyboard, you'll see tiny numbers and mathematical symbols in a different color on the keys under your right hand (U, I, O, P, etc., as shown below).

If you hold down the **fn** key, this embedded **numeric keypad** becomes active. Use these numbers as you would in any application on any Mac, such as a spreadsheet or the calculator. You have to keep the fn key down to use the numbers.

You *do* have a Numeric Keypad

Some programs, such as Microsoft Word and Adobe PageMaker, have always utilized the numeric keypad for moving the cursor, and you have to turn on num lock if you want to type numbers. On the iBook keyboard, these keys can't do both (move the cursor and type numbers), so in Word and PageMaker, when the fn key is down and num lock is on, the cursor moves— you don't get the numeric keypad.

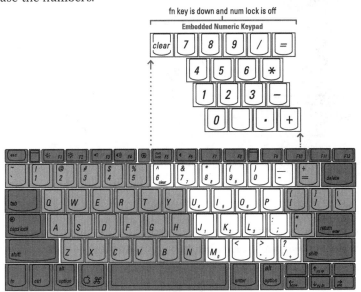

With **fn** key down, the rest of the keys on the keyboard retain their original functions, as shown above, and you have to hold down the **fn** key as you type numbers. However, press the **num lock key** (F5), and all other keys are disabled *except* for the numeric keypad, and you don't have to hold the **fn** key down as you type numbers.

Num Lock

num lock is on

Keyboard Control Panel

Keyboard

The Keyboard control panel (shown below, left) has a button labeled "Function Keys…." Click it to open the "Hot Function Keys" window, shown below.

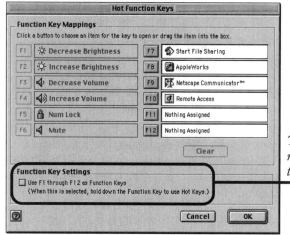

The "Function Key" mentioned here refers to the **fn** *key.*

The "Function Key Settings" checkbox lets you determine whether the **fn** key has to be held down for the hot keys to function.

♦ If the box is **unchecked,** the Control Buttons and the hot keys you've assigned work **without** holding down the **fn** key.

♦ If you **check** the box, you have to hold down the **fn** key to get the Control Buttons and the hot keys to work, and to turn Num Lock on or off. (If you **check** the box, the Control Buttons F1–F4 become the standard Undo, Cut, Copy, and Paste buttons as on any other Mac.)

This window does not affect any of the other function keys, such as the numeric keypad or the modifier keys—it affects only the keys F1–F12.

Are you typing extra characters?

If you find that you type extra letters all the time because you tend to hold your finger on the keys a little too long, open the Keyboard control panel and change the "Delay Until Repeat" to either the shortest length or off.

Removing the Keyboard Cover

The **keyboard cover** can be easily removed so you can install more RAM (memory) or an AirPort Card or just peek inside. To make the inside of the iBook less accessible to youngsters, turn the little screw set between the F4 and F5 keys to "lock" the keyboard shut. For details on opening the keyboard cover, see Chapter 1.

Connecting to the Internet 4

You have all the software you need on the iBook to connect to the Internet. The one thing that's missing from the iBook is an **Internet service provider,** which is a company that connects *your* computer to the vast network of computers that makes the Internet and the World Wide Web. You have three options if you're not on a corporate network:

- ♦ **A local Internet service provider:** Call your friends in town and ask who they use locally for their Internet connection. Try to find a provider who is familiar with Macs. Call them up.

- ♦ **EarthLink.** The list of national service providers has boiled down to two (and they're merging)—EarthLink and MindSpring. A national provider can give you access codes all over the country, so if you travel with your iBook a lot, you might want to use EarthLink or MindSpring (or AOL, if you want their services).

- ♦ **America Online:** If you choose to use AOL (see Chapter 2 for a description of America Online) then you can ignore all references to an ISP (Internet service provider). AOL *is* your service provider, your Internet connection, and even your web browser all rolled into one neat package for $19.95 a month. If you choose AOL, you can even ignore the rest of this entire chapter. Go double-click on the America Online icon, follow the directions, and you're on. Goodbye.

    America Online

    If you have an ISP for yourself, but someone else in your family wants to use AOL, AOL has a special price if you go through your own ISP (see the America Online information in Chapter 2).

Where to Begin

If you are not connected to the Internet at all yet, read through this chapter up through page 85 (where it begins to talk about control panels and other features specifically) so you have an overall view of the process. If you are totally unfamiliar with the World Wide Web, the Internet, email, and the concept of "connecting," you might want to read the Internet sections in either *The Little iMac Book* or *The Little Mac Book*. Or barrel blindly ahead with glee—you'll figure it out!

The Internet Setup Assistant opens the very first time you turn on your iBook. After that, go to the Apple menu, slide down to "Internet Access," and choose "Internet Setup Assistant."

Mac OS 8.5 and above has something called the **Internet Setup Assistant** that walks you through getting yourself connected to the Internet. You must first have made a decision whether you are going to use America Online, a local Internet service provider (an ISP), EarthLink, or the network connection at work, as explained on the opposite page.

After the section about getting your connection established, the rest of this chapter explains the individual control panels and dialog boxes on your iBook where you can customize settings. If you get your connection working and everything is fine, don't mess with anything else unless you find a need. You might want to read through that information just so you have a better understanding of what all these things are.

You Need a Modem

Of course, before you can get connected in the first place, you must have a modem or other means of connecting to the Internet. Your iBook has a built-in (internal) 56K modem. The phone jack on the left side of your iBook is where you connect the iBook to your telephone line. Don't get the modem port mixed up with the Ethernet port! The modem port is exactly the size of a regular phone cable; the Ethernet port looks very similar, but it's larger—a phone cable won't snap into it neatly. Just plug one end of a phone cable directly into the modem port, and the other end of the cable into the wall jack or into another phone.

If your phone won't take another cable, go to a local office supply store and buy a phone doubler, a little $5 attachment that goes into the one wall jack and gives you two jacks to plug cables into. Then you can connect both your phone and your modem cable into the same line.

This is the little phone doubler you can buy so you can plug two devices into the one wall jack.

If you are lucky enough to have a fast connection like cable, T1, or DSL (Digital Subscriber Line), then you'll use an Ethernet cable and the Ethernet port: plug the Ethernet cable (which looks like a phone cable but with bigger connectors on the ends) into the Ethernet port on the iBook, and the other end into the special box you'll have for the fast line. Someone will come set up this sort of connection for you.

The **Internet Setup Assistant** facilitates connecting you to an Internet service provider. There are two important things to know before you jump into this Setup Assistant:

1. **If you are using America Online as your Internet connection, you do not need to use this Internet Setup Assistant at all.** Ignore it. Double-click the AOL icon and close this book.

2. If you are not using America Online, or you are using it but you want a direct Internet connection *in addition* to AOL, **you must first establish a relationship with an Internet service provider.** A "relationship" means you either **a)** call up a local or national ISP (Internet service provider), tell them you want to connect to the Internet through their service, register yourself with them, and pay them money. They will give you all the strange information you need to enter into this Internet Setup Assistant.

   Or **b)** if you don't want to use a *local* ISP, the Internet Setup Assistant will give you a national provider option (EarthLink). Have your credit card handy, and you can register during the setup process. All of the strange information will be entered for you automatically and you can just log on right away.

   Or **c)** if you are in an office and use a LAN (local area network, meaning your computers are all in the same office complex or building), talk to your network supervisor instead of an ISP.

To use the Internet Setup Assistant

1. If the Assistant is already open and in front of you, go to Step **2.**

   If the alias to the Internet Setup Assistant is sitting on your Desktop, double-click it.

   If you don't see the Internet Setup Assistant icon (it's usually in a folder called "Assistants"), use Sherlock's Find File (Command F at the Desktop) to find it for you. Double-click it.

Internet Setup Assistant

This is the icon you want to double-click to start the process.

2. The first window that appears is this one you see to the right. Since you have gotten this far, you most likely want to click "Yes."

3. This is an important question.

Answer **No** if you have never had your own connection to the Internet on any computer, **or** if you want to make *another* one. For instance, you might have America Online but you also want a direct connection to the Internet. Or two people use the same computer and each pay for their own Internet connection separately. *Continue to* **Step 4A,** *below, and follow the "A" steps.*

Answer **Yes** if: You have/had an individual connection on another computer, either at home or work, and you want to establish that same connection on this computer. **Or** you contacted a local or national ISP and set up a relationship with them and you have the appropriate information to enter. **Or** you are on a local network (LAN), as is typical in a large office environment, and want to connect this computer to that network. *Skip to* **Step 4B** *(page 81) and follow the "B" steps.*

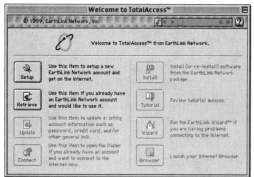

4A. The TotalAccess Assistant takes you step-by-step through the setup of a new or existing account with EarthLink Network on your iBook.

EarthLink can be a great solution if you are in a city in which EarthLink offers a local phone number and you are in the contiguous United States. At the moment the basic service is $19.95 a month, but if you live in Hawaii or Alaska, expect to pay an extra $9 PER HOUR on top of that. If EarthLink doesn't have a local phone number in your area (which is very likely if you live in someplace like New Mexico or Arkansas), you can ask for an 800 number which costs $6 PER HOUR extra (check for current pricing).

You can follow this process through to the point of checking for local phone numbers in EarthLink (Step 6A), and if they don't have one for you, you can cancel the process with no harm done. If you decide EarthLink isn't the best solution for you, call a connected friend or computer consultant and ask about local providers.

Click the "Setup" button to set up a new account, or click the "Retrieve" button to set up your existing EarthLink Network account on your new iBook.

EarthLink does have great and wonderful tech support 24 hours a day, and the service is pretty good and very convenient. If this is your first Internet connection and you're anxious to connect and don't want to shop around, EarthLink is a very good choice.

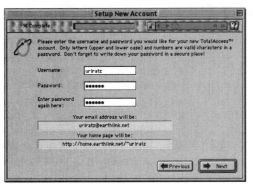

5A. Enter a Username. Try to make the Username unique. When you register, EarthLink will check to see if your Username is already being used by someone; if so, you'll have to change yours at that point.

Use letters and numbers, and don't put any spaces in the Username.

Your password should be something you'll remember, but write it down and keep it in a safe place anyway. Many passwords are "case sensitive," which means it's very important if you use capital letters or not, so remember exactly how you spelled your password, including caps and lowercase.

6A. You'll be guided through several other self-explanatory dialog boxes. Just fill them in. Eventually you'll get a TotalAccess message alerting you that your iBook is going to dial an 800 number. It uses your modem to do this, so make sure your modem's plugged into a phone connection (or whatever sort of connection you use). Click OK.

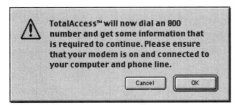

7A. You'll get a Product Info window with pricing and product description information. You've made no commitment yet, so if you decide you don't want to use EarthLink, you can quit now (press Command Q).

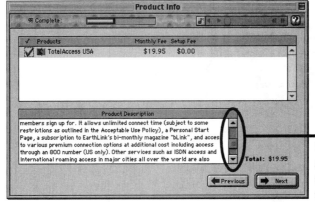

Use the scroll arrows to slide the information up and down so you can read it all.

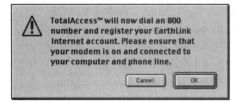

8A. Finally, you'll see a message window alerting you that TotalAccess will again dial an 800 number and register your EarthLink Internet account. You'll end up at the EarthLink home page, which will look something like the one shown below, but it will be customized for you.

9A. EarthLink makes a "Personal Start Page" for you. When you connect to the Internet, your browser will open and your Personal Start Page will appear in front of you. When you get email, there will be a message on that page. Find the link that says something about your email, and click it. Whatever email application you set as your default in the Internet control panel (see page 87) will open and you can read and send your messages.

If you chose the EarthLink account, you're done with this section. Skip to page 85 and read how to log on, read pages 86–88 about the Internet control panel, and then skim the rest of the chapter. When you need the information that's in the rest of the chapter, it will be here waiting for you. Until then, you can ignore it.

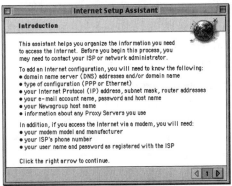

4B. So if you are at this dialog box it means you have the information ready to plug into these dialog boxes. If you are **not** on a LAN (local area network, like in a corporation or large office), you won't need to know your IP address, subnet mask, and route addresses (whatever those are). If you **are** on a network, make sure you get that information from your network supervisor because you will be asked to enter it.

Important note: The **user name and password as registered with the ISP** is NOT the same as your name and password for your email!! Often the ISP assigns you a user name and password and you might not even know what it is. Be very sure to ask specifically for this information.

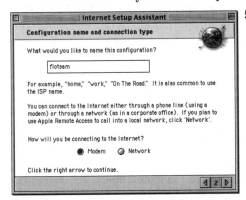

5B. The name of the **configuration** (the connection specifications you are about to set up) should be something you would recognize in a list, such as the name of the person to whom the account belongs, or perhaps the name of the provider.

If you are using the company network, click the "Network" button. Some of the windows you see will look different from the ones shown here because you have to enter other information.

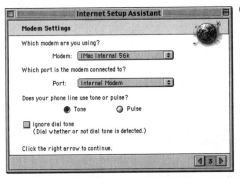

6B. Press on the **Modem** menu for a big list of modems you might have connected. If you don't find exactly your modem, choose one by the same manufacturer, or try one of the Hayes models.

If your modem is internal, choose that option for the **Port.** If it's not internal, choose the "Modem port" option unless you specifically know you should choose something else.

Most modern phones use **Tone.** If you have a pushbutton phone, it's tone. If you have an old phone that dials, it's **Pulse** (and it's not great for data transfer over the Internet).

You might want to **Ignore dial tone** if you're calling through some kind of phone system that uses a dial tone that a modem won't recognize (more common overseas).

If you have **call waiting** service, you must enter *70 to turn it off while you are connected because if you are online and someone calls you, your call waiting will disconnect you from the Internet.

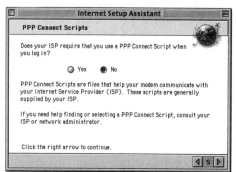

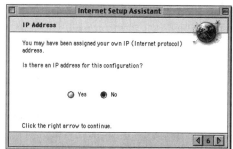

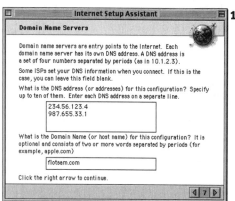

7B. Your service provider gives you the **phone number** you need. This is the number your *computer* will call to connect to the ISP; this is not the number *you* use to call your ISP on the phone!

The **log in name** or **user ID** and the **password,** as I mentioned in Step 4B, are not the same as your name and password for your email! Be sure to get the specific name and password that the ISP has registered to you for connectivity.

8B. Unless your service provider told you that you need a script and gave you a script file, click "No" here and move on. If your ISP did give you a script file, drop it on top of the closed System Folder; the iBook will put the script into the Modem Scripts folder for you. Ask your ISP how they want you to use it.

9B. Unless you are logged on to a dedicated line that is open all the time, like on a network in a large corporation or college setting, you will not have your own **IP address.** Actually, your home or small office computer *will* have an IP address when you log on, but the number of that address will change just about every time you log on. If you *are* on a network, ask your network supervisor for your IP address.

10B. Your ISP will give you this information. They'll probably give you at least two different **DNS addresses.** Type the first one in, then hit a Return to type the second one. It's a good idea to write these numbers down somewhere because I guarantee someday you will have to type them into some other dialog box.

The **domain name** or **host name** is often the same as your email *account* name (see the note in 11B).

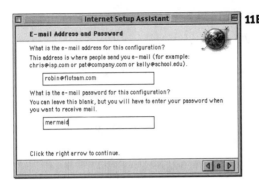

11B. Notice the difference between this window and the next one: this one asks for your **email address** and the next one asks for your **email account.** In many cases these are the same, but sometimes they're not. For instance, my real email **account** is robin@nets.com through a connection with a local ISP called studio x. But I bought the domain ratz.com and I have a web site at ratz.com, so my email **address** that I give out is robin@ratz.com. The ratz *address,* however, actually gets routed through my *account* at nets.com. If you've just set up your account with your ISP and they gave you an email address, then you will enter the same thing in both this window and the next one, unless they tell you differently. Ask if your email address is the same as your email account.

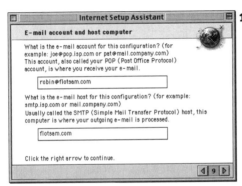

12B. Your ISP will give you the correct information for this window. Take note of the "SMTP" host; you'll run into that term again and it's good to know the name of your SMTP host. It will make you feel powerful and smart, too, to be able to name your SMTP host when you need it.

13B. Newsgroups are like public bulletin boards where people post messages about certain topics. Because there are almost 30,000 different newsgroups, few ISPs can store the information for all of them. Many ISPs have arrangements with another server (a host) to allow their users to access the other servers' newsgroups. Even that host may not have every newsgroup; if they don't have the one you want, you can always ask them to carry a particular one for you. It shouldn't cost anything.

Your ISP will tell you what to enter here. You don't have to enter anything if you think you won't be using newsgroups, and if you change your mind later, you can always add a host name in the Internet control panel (see page 87).

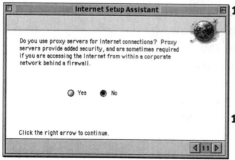

14B. Unless, as it states, you are on something like a corporate or university network, click "No" here. If you *are* on a high-end network, ask your network supervisor which button you should choose.

15B. When you get to the next window, click the button **Show Details** (it turns into "Hide Details" after you click it). It's a good idea to keep track of this information. An easy way to capture this info is to make a screen shot of this window and print it up:

a. Press Caps Lock down.

b. Hold the Command and Shift keys down, and tap the number 4. Your pointer will turn into a big, round dot, like this: ●

c. With that big, round dot, click right on the Internet Setup Assistant window. You'll hear a crashing sound, I mean, you'll hear the sound of a picture being taken.

Go ahead and finish up the connection process: click the "Go Ahead" button (you'll print the window in a minute, after you're done here). The iBook has filled in all the necessary control panels with this information so everything is all set. Read the next page about logging on and logging off.

Picture 1

To print the window with all of that important information: Look in your hard disk window. There's a file called Picture 1. Double-click it and it will open in SimpleText. From the File menu, choose "Print." Click OK. Be sure to fill in the actual passwords before you forget them!!

Logging On to the Internet

There are a number of ways to log on and off of the Internet. You'll find the one that suits you best. It's generally recommended that you establish a connection first, and then open your browser or email software, rather than open the browser or email software and let it make a connection. Here are several options for connecting:

♦ If you use **America Online,** just double-click the AOL icon. If you want to use a different browser, then after you are logged on with AOL , double-click the alias of your preferred browser (an alias that you previously made and put on the Desktop for this purpose). Skip the rest of these ideas.

AOL

OR: If you still have the icon on your Desktop called **Browse the Internet,** just double-click it. It will connect you and also open the browser you have selected in the Internet control panel (see next page).

Browse the Internet

OR: In the Apple menu is a choice called **Remote Access Status.** Choose it and you get the dialog box shown below, left. Click the "Connect" button, and after your connection is established, double-click your browser icon.

While you are connected, this box provides information to you, and the little bubbles indicate the activity going on. Notice you can disconnect from here.

OR: If your **Control Strip** is showing, use the Remote Access button (below, right). Click it to get the pop-up menu. If you have made more than one configuration, choose the one you want. Then click the icon again, and this time click "Connect."

OR: You might have a **menu item** in the upper-right of your screen for connecting. If you do and you like that, use it.

When you quit the browser, that does not automatically disconnect you! Use the Remote Access control panel (pages 90–91) to make your connection automatically disconnect if there's been no activity after a specified amount of time. Manually **disconnect** using the Remote Access Status bar or the Remote Access button on the Control Strip, both shown above.

Logging off

If your Apple icon is alternating with this Remote Access icon, it means you are connected!

Internet Control Panel

This is the greatest invention. This one single control panel will make things so much easier for you. Not only can you set up defaults for your email, browser, etc., but you can make different sets for different situations or people (choose "New Set…" from the File menu), then change sets with the click of a button. You'll become well acquainted with this control panel. If, when you first open it, it's closed up like the one shown below, click on the tiny arrow next to "Edit Sets."

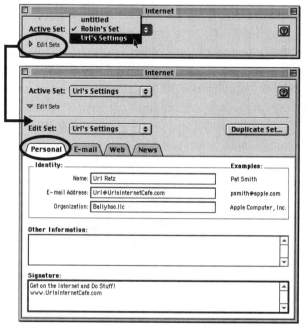

If you went through the Internet Setup Assistant, most of this information was entered for you.

Personal settings

Finger *is a program that lets anyone see if you're online, how long you've been online, when you were last online, your user ID, your full name, PLUS any information you type into this "Other Information" box. Typically colleges, universities, and corporations have set up a finger facility. You can go to "finger gateways" on the web, type in the email address of anyone, and you might get something back. Many ISPs opt not to supply this information on their servers, and other ISPs might set up information* **for** *you that someone can finger. Check with your ISP to see what their policy is. America Online does not provide finger information on any of their customers.*

Other Information is where you can type anything you want people to know about you if they "finger" you (see the sidebar explanation).

Anything you type in the **Signature** box will automatically show up at the end of every email you send and every news message you post. You've surely seen signatures in every one else's emails. They can be very elaborate with little pictures made of typed characters, or they might advertise your web site or latest book, provide your postal mail address and phone number, or make a statement about your philosophy of life.

The "E-Mail" section is pretty self-explanatory. Notice in the example below that I've chosen the endearing AOL "You've Got Mail" as the sound that plays to tell me there's mail, even though I use Eudora (another email application). I found the sound in the AOL folder and put a copy into my System file, and then it shows up in this menu.

E-mail settings

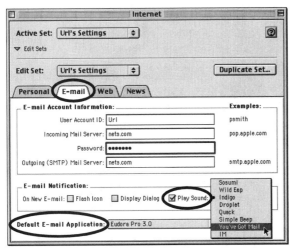

If you went through the Internet Setup Assistant, most of this information was entered for you.

This "Default E-mail Application" is an important option for you to check. Whatever you choose here will open when you double-click the Mail icon.

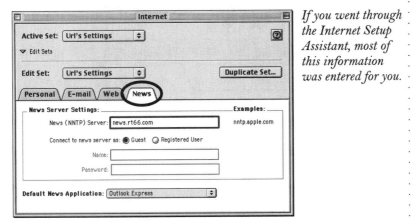

If you went through the Internet Setup Assistant, most of this information was entered for you.

News settings

See Step 13B on page 83 about newsgroups. Outlook Express, which is on your iBook, is a great application for viewing and posting to newsgroups.

Web settings
The Web settings let you set a **Home Page** and a **Search Page** for when you click the Home or Search buttons in your browser toolbar. However, most browsers use their own preferences (which you can also set; choose "Preferences…" from the Edit menu in your browser) rather than these in the Internet control panel. The same goes for **Colors & Links.**

You can create your own folder and have all of your downloaded files go directly into this folder; use the **Download Files To** option. Again, your browser might override your setup here; check and see.

The most important choice for you, though, is the **Default Web Browser.** This one actually works great. On your iBook you have both Netscape Communicator and Microsoft Internet Explorer. Whichever one you choose here is what will open when you click the icons "Browse the Internet" or "Connect to…."

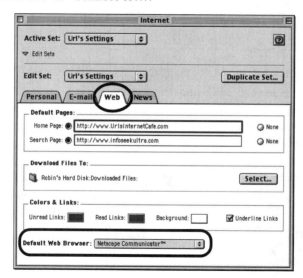

Of course, to connect to the Internet you need a **modem** of some sort. Your iBook has a 56K internal modem, and all you do is plug a phone cord into the side of the iBook and then into the phone jack in the wall. If you need to, you can plug the cord into a phone, and then the phone's cord into the wall, but if you have a wall jack handy, you can go straight in.

The **Modem control panel** is pretty self-explanatory:

- ◆ In the "Connect via" area, the default is "Internal Modem." If you install an AirPort Card for wireless connectivity, this option will change so you could choose to connect via the internal modem or the wireless connection.

- ◆ From the "Modem" list, choose what's called a modem script. It's best to use the default "Apple Internal 56K Modem (v.90)."

- ◆ Make your "Sound" choice: Turn the modem squeal on or off as you like. Sometimes you might like it on so you know it's actually trying to work; other times you might like it off so no one knows you're connecting.

- ◆ Make your "Dialing" choice: If your phone has push buttons, it's most likely tone. If you have to dial around the numbers, it's pulse (which is not great for connecting).

- ◆ Close the control panel. You'll be asked to save the changes; click the "Save" button.

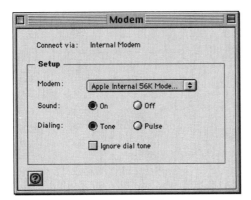

Modem Control Panel

Modem

If you used the Internet Setup Assistant, it filled in the Modem control panel for you.

Remote Access Control Panel

*If America Online is your only Internet access, you don't need to open this control panel because AOL **is** your telecommunications software!*

You need two things to connect to the Internet: a modem and some sort of telecommunications software. There are software packages you can buy for general telecommunications, but your iBook has Remote Access, which gets you connected to the Internet quite nicely. The **Remote Access control panel** used to be called PPP (which stands for point-to-point protocol) so if this looks familiar to you, it is.

If you went through the Mac Internet Setup Assistant (pages 77–84), the Remote Access control panel is already filled in with your settings. You only need to open this if you need to make individual changes in your settings, or if you are feeling like an Advanced User and want to make extra "configurations," or collections of settings, that you can apply with the click of a button. For instance, if you are traveling with your iBook and want to change the specifications for the hotel you're in, but you don't want to lose your home specs, you can make a new configuration while saving your old one.

You can also use this control panel to connect to the Internet. Generally, though, you'll use one of the other methods mentioned on page 85 to make the connection.

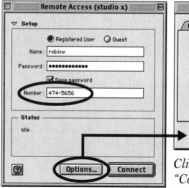 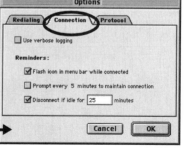

Sometimes your ISP will give you more than one phone number to use, in case one is busy. If so, you can replace the one in the "Number" field, then connect to that new number (but keep both numbers written down in a safe place!).

Click the Options button, then click the "Connection" tab to get this dialog box. The default is to flash the icon in the menu bar while connected, which is a good reminder. This is where you can determine the amount of time Remote Access should wait until it automatically disconnects you from the Internet. If you choose a prompt, a dialog box will appear on your screen asking if you want to stay connected. You might hear a man or lady read the message out loud to you (if this makes you crazy, see page 183).

To make a new Remote Access configuration, you have to duplicate an existing one, rename it, and make changes to it. So:

1. Open the Remote Access control panel, if it isn't already (from the Apple menu, slide down to Control Panels, then choose "Remote Access").

2. From the File menu, choose "Configurations...."

3. To make a new configuration, select any other one and click "Duplicate...." Name the new one (this name will appear in the Remote Access control strip menu). If you want this new one active so you can make changes to the specifications, click "Make Active."

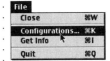

Use the RemoteAccess menu to call up each of the other control panels in which you might want to change specs. You can only get to Dial-Assist if you first change the User Mode to Advanced (use the Edit menu to do that). DialAssist lets you enter different numbers for different parts of the world, or use a calling card in a hotel room.

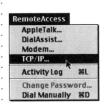

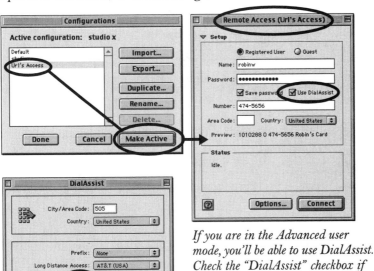

This is the Remote Access menu. From here you can access the other control panels, as listed above, to change their specs. Unfortunately, these individual changes cannot be retained in one global configuration.

If you are in the Advanced user mode, you'll be able to use DialAssist. Check the "DialAssist" checkbox if you want your connection process to use the numbers you set up in there.

Each of the menus here in DialAssist can be customized if you click on their matching buttons. Check it out— it's quite self-explanatory. For details on how to enter prefixes and suffixes, including commas to force pauses, see the information in the FAXstf software, pages 46–47.

TCP/IP Control Panel

The control panel called TCP/IP sounds and looks a little intimidating, but what TCP/IP does is actually quite interesting. You see, when we send an email message, in our minds we picture a little letter going through the phone lines and landing in someone else's computer. What actually happens is that the email message you write gets chopped up into little pieces called packets, all these packets go through the phone lines on different routes, and they're all put back together again at the other end. TCP is the layer of the program that divides the email file into the individual packets and numbers them. TCP then sends the packets to the IP layer of the program. The IP sends the packets on their way, sending each one in a different direction, and the packets stop at all kinds of computers along their paths, asking directions to make sure they're still going the right way. At the other computer, TCP puts all the packets back together again in the right order. Once they're all reassembled correctly, it sends the single file to your mailbox. Amazingly, the same thing happens to web pages coming to you. Once you see how busy and important these little TCP and IP workers are, this dialog box isn't so intimidating.

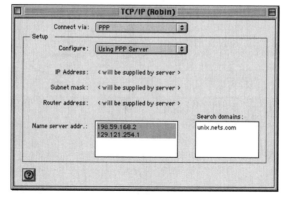

No one expects you to know what the correct choices are for this dialog box. Your ISP or network administrator (if you're in a networked office or school) has to tell you these things. If you used the Internet Setup Assistant, this dialog box was filled out for you automatically with this information as you supplied it.

You may have heard a lot of hoopla about Apple's **Personal Web Sharing.** The concept is that you can put a folder of items, including but not limited to web pages, on your Desktop, and anyone can see the files on *your* Desktop by using *their* browser at *their* computer. If the files are web pages, the other person can look at the web pages just like they look at any web site. If the files are text documents, the other person can read the text. Personal web sharing can go hand in hand with Apple's file sharing (see Chapter 5), with the added advantage that people who are not on your local network can view the files, and people who are using computers other than Macintosh can view the files.

The one most important aspect to understand about this technology is that it is meant for people who are either connected through a LAN (local area network, such as an entire office complex), or people who have a connection that stays on 24 hours a day, such as a digital or cable connection.

If you use a modem and dial in to an Internet service provider, don't bother using Personal Web Sharing. For people to get to your web site through Personal Web Sharing, you have to be connected to the Internet (or your LAN) at the time the person tries to find your web pages, *and* you have to give them a special "IP address" (Internet Protocol, shown below). When you use a modem to dial in to a server, your IP address is different just about every time. The only way someone could get to the web sharing folder on your hard disk is if you connect to your service provider, open the Web Sharing control panel to turn on web sharing and see what the address is for that moment, call the person who wants to get to your folder, tell them the address, and have them connect to the Internet, enter the address, and get to your folder before your dial-up connection drops or you get disconnected for some reason.

Personal Web Sharing

Web Sharing

This is the Web Sharing control panel that enables other people to see your folder through the Internet or an intranet.

A web address, or URL, is the address to a particular web page; an IP address is the address to a particular computer.

—continued

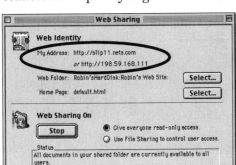

Above is where you'd find the IP address you must give someone who wants to connect to share your web folder.

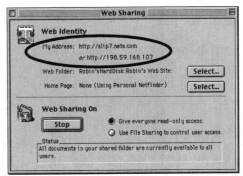

Here you can see that the IP address I had (left) has changed because I got disconnected and had to log on again.

An intranet
vs. the Internet
intra = within
inter = between

You might notice that most of the Apple documentation refers to Personal Web Sharing as "the easiest way to share your information with everyone on your **intranet,**" that you can make your pages "available to everyone in your **organization,**" and that you can "give your address to the people on your **intranet.**" An intranet is different from the Internet. An intranet is a closed network, usually computers within a single office or company that are all connected (networked) and that network is not available to outside viewers. It's possible for companies to have a network that spans states or countries or continents (a WAN, or wide area network), but what is on their intranet is still accessible only to privileged users. The reason Personal Web Sharing is best suited for an intranet is because the network is always on so your computer's IP address never changes.

The basic steps to
Personal Web Sharing

Understanding the limitations of Personal Web Sharing, you might still want to do it, either to show a friend or client something over the Internet, or because you are connected to a LAN or a constant high-speed connection. There are many variables to this web sharing stuff, so the best thing to do is read the directions. Read the manual. Read the documentation that's installed on your hard disk with the rest of the Personal Web Sharing files (use Sherlock's Find File to search for "About Personal WebSharing," with "websharing" as one word). Basically, this is what to do:

Robin's Web Site

1. Make a folder that will store the files (shown to the left).

2. In this folder put the files you want to share, the web pages you want to post, or both (shown to the left).

3. If your network connection is not already up and running, connect to it now.

4. Open the Web Sharing control panel (shown below).

5. Click the first "Select" button and tell Web Sharing which folder you want to share.

6. Click the second "Select" button and tell Web Sharing the name of the web page you want to appear as the default, the home page. If you choose "None," then the visitor will see a list of the files in the folder (as shown on the next page).

7. Click the "Start" button to start the web sharing process.

This is the Web Sharing control panel.

8. Notice in the control panel there is a web address in the first line, "My address." Write it down—this is your **IP address,** the address of your computer where your shared file is stored. This is the address you give to anyone who wants to use their browser to surf over to your web site. If you see two addresses, use either one.

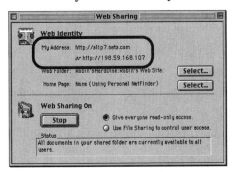

9. If you chose a web page as the Home Page, then when a visitor gets to your folder that web page is what they will see in their browser. If you chose "None," they will see something like this:

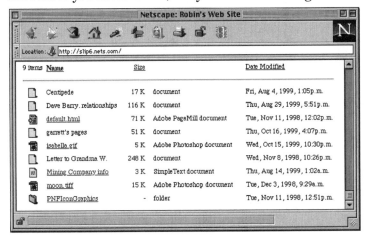

The files that appear as links in this browser window will open to display the graphic or the text. The files that do not appear as links cannot be opened through the browser.

If you experiment with serving a web page from your computer with a dial-up connection, you must remove the alias of the Web Sharing control panel from the Startup Items Folder in the System Folder when you're done. If you don't, every time you turn on your Mac the Web Sharing will try to kick in, causing potential problems. If you have trouble, restart, hold down the Spacebar until the Extensions Manager appears, then uncheck "Web Sharing" from the Startup Items Folder. Click "Continue."

You have to make a proper web page if you want to use one as a home page. If you are interested in making web pages, read **The Non-Designer's Web Book,** *by John and Robin.*

Important Note

Use the Help Files!

Oh, this Internet stuff can be so confusing, especially to set it up, and there are so many variables. Don't forget about the Help files. They are sometimes actually helpful. From the Help menu at the Desktop, choose "Mac OS Help," or press Command ?.

Click one of the headings in the left panel, and subheadings will appear in the right panel. Or type in a word or phrase at the top of the window, then click "Search."

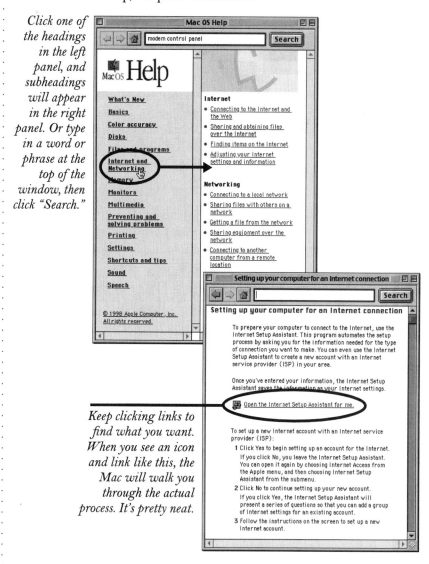

Keep clicking links to find what you want. When you see an icon and link like this, the Mac will walk you through the actual process. It's pretty neat.

Sharing Files 5

Chances are your iBook is not the only computer in your life. If you have other Macintoshes in your home or office, you can set them all up to share files. This makes it so easy to work with others on projects, keep files updated on both computers, send documents back and forth, and more.

You can connect two computers together with Ethernet cables and set up the control panels to share in about five minutes. Then sending files back and forth is as easy as dropping a file into a special folder on one computer, and it shows up on the other computer.

If you buy a wireless card to insert into your iBook, you can set up one iBook or an AirPort Base Station to act as an "access point," and up to ten other computers that have wireless cards can share files without any cables at all.

File Sharing Software You need to have installed and turned on the **file sharing software** that came with your iBook. It's probably already there—open the Extensions Manager (find it in the Apple menu, under Control Panels) and look for the control panels *Apple Talk*, *File Sharing*, and *Users & Groups*, plus the extensions *AppleShare*, *File Sharing Extension*, and *File Sharing Library*. Make sure they each have a checkmark in their little boxes. If they are in the list but don't have checkmarks, check them and restart.

If some of those items aren't in the Extensions Manager list at all, they're apparently not installed. You can run the Installer again from your original CD that came with your Mac (have that power user friend of yours help you). In the Installer, click "Customize," and choose those items that are missing.

AppleTalk and Ethernet The Mac has the **AppleTalk** networking software built into it that allows you to connect with other kinds of networks.

Ethernet is a much faster connection than AppleTalk. Your iBook, as well as most new Macs such as G3s, iMacs, and the more expensive PowerBooks, have Ethernet ports. It looks like the phone jack, but it's bigger.

An Ethernet connection might be what's called 10BASE-T or 100BASE-T, both of which refer to how fast the information travels through the wires. 100BASE-T is, of course, faster than 10BASE-T. The iBook, the iMac, and the translucent blue G3s have 10/100BASE-T Ethernet ports, which means they are really 100BASE-T but you can connect them to other Macs that have slower 10BASE-T connections.

AirPort Wireless The iBook is capable of a **wireless network,** which means you can log on to the Internet and share files with other computers with literally no wires attached to the computer. But to do this you have to buy an AirPort Base Station (about $300) and/or an AirPort Card (about $100) to insert into each iBook. See pages 111–114 for details.

You have a Network! Once you have connected two or more computers, you have created what is called a **LAN,** or local area network.

The first thing you must do before you can actually share files is connect the two computers together with a cable.* If you have bought and installed the AirPort system, see the note below, then skip to Step 2.

Ethernet port

A. Connect two computers directly to each other using an Ethernet cable and Ethernet ports for a fast connection (for instance, iBook to iBook or iBook to G3). The AirPort wireless network is even faster.

AAUI port

B. If the computer you need to connect the iBook to does not have an Ethernet port, it probably has what's called an AAUI port. You'll recognize it by this symbol, **<•••>**, which is the same symbol above an Ethernet port.

If the other computer has an AAUI port, you need to buy an adapter, called a transceiver, so you can plug the Ethernet cable into it. You can buy one from any Mac catalog or large office supply and computer stores.

You have to buy the **Ethernet cables.** In buying Ethernet cables, the most common type is "twisted pair, cat 3 or cat 5" (cat 5 is more protected and is usually used in professional networking situations). You need to make sure the cable is what's called "crossover."

In buying a **transceiver** for a Mac that doesn't have an Ethernet port, the most common is a "10BASE-T transceiver," although 100BASE-T is rapidly becoming very common. Make sure you buy a transceiver that is compliant with your computer.

*If you have bought and installed a wireless networking system, you won't need to connect the wireless-enabled computers with a cable. But you will need to:

♦ Install the software that came with your wireless system (see pages 111–114 for information about Apple's AirPort).

♦ Configure an extra control panel with choices like "ad hoc network" or "peer-to-peer network."

♦ Configure your TCP/IP control panel.

Because the AirPort system doesn't come out until several months after this book is published, we can't give you any more details than that! We're very sorry, but you'll have to read the directions.

Once you have your system set up, the steps in the rest of the chapter to share files should be the same.

STEP 1: Connect the Computers

For almost any connectivity solution, check out Farallon at **www.farallon.com.** *They are constantly coming up with new products to make connections and networking easier and faster no matter what arrangement of computers you might have.*

Buying Ethernet cables

Buying a transceiver

Wireless networking
Even if you have a wireless system installed in your iBook, if you want to network with another computer that is **not** *enabled for wireless networking, you'll still have to use cables.*

STEP 2:
Turn AppleTalk On

Before you begin to connect, make sure **AppleTalk is turned on** or nothing will work anyway. Turn it on on both computers.

♦ From the Apple menu, slide down to Control Panels, then choose "AppleTalk."

♦ If you don't see an "Options…" button, go to the Edit menu, choose "User Mode…," click the "Advanced" button. Click OK.

♦ Click the "Options…" button.

♦ If it isn't already on, click the "Active" button.

♦ Don't close the AppleTalk control panel yet . . .

Apple recommends that you use this control panel when you need to turn off AppleTalk. **Don't** *use the Chooser or the Control Strip to turn AppleTalk off.*

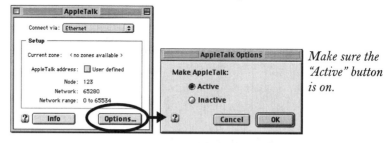

Make sure the "Active" button is on.

STEP 3:
Choose Your Connection Method

Check the AppleTalk control panel and make sure it's set to the correct choice, depending on whether you are using Ethernet cables (plugged into the Ethernet ports) or a wireless connection (both computers have wireless cards installed). Do this on both computers.

♦ If it's not already open, open the control panel "AppleTalk."

♦ Choose "Ethernet."

♦ To close this control panel, click in the little close box. It will ask if you want to save these changes; click "Save."

If you are using a wireless network, you'll have a wireless option here in this menu. Choose it.

Note: You have to come back to this dialog box when you need to use another connection. For instance, on my G3 I choose Ethernet when I want to share files with my iBook, but when I want to print directly to my laser printer (which uses LocalTalk), I have to open this AppleTalk control panel again and switch to "Printer." (In the iBook example above, LocalTalk isn't even an option because there is no LocalTalk.)

Now you must **name the Macintosh** and the owner. Generally the biggest computer will be your *file server*, or the one to which the iBook will connect. In large offices or school labs, there are one or more computers that do nothing except act as file servers. In your home or small office, one of the Macs will be considered the file server, but to you it will still be your working Mac.

Name the Macintosh (we're going to refer to this serving Mac as **Mac A**) through the File Sharing control panel:

a. From your Apple menu, slide down to Control Panels, then choose "File Sharing." The control panel is shown below.

b. Type your name in the edit box "Owner Name."

c. Make up a password, up to eight characters, which will give you control over whether other people have access to your files. After you type your password, the letters turn into bullets, like so: (••••). Remember this password!

d. Type a name for your Mac (this is still **Mac A**). This is the name that the person on the other computer (Mac B) needs to know to connect to you. This name will appear in their Chooser when they try to connect to your computer. If you are connecting several Macs together, create memorable and distinct names. Notice I named this one "Robin's Hard Disk." Very creative.

e. Click the "Start" button to turn File Sharing on. (If the button says "Stop," then file sharing is already on—don't click it!)

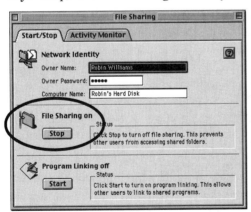

f. Click the close box to put this control panel away.

File Sharing
control panel

File Sharing

If you ever do forget your password, follow Step 6 to set up a Guest user; a Guest doesn't need a password.

Turn on file sharing

After you click the "Start" button, that button turns into "Stop." Notice the message above the Stop button now says "File Sharing on." Notice also that the folder has wires coming out the side, a visual clue that information is flowing in and out of the folder.

"Program Linking" allows other users on your network to link to applications that are sharable. Not all applications are sharable, and most applications that can be shared must be first set up for sharing, which often includes paying a higher fee for the program if more than one computer is going to use it.

STEP 5:
Make a Folder
to Share

Make a new folder on **Mac A** *or* select an existing folder and give this folder sharing privileges (instructions below). Mac B users will be able to see this folder on their hard disk, they can see anything inside of it, and they can put items into this folder on their own computer; the files they put in this folder will show up on your **Mac A.**

a. Click on a folder to select it. You can select more than one folder at a time.

b. From the File menu, slide down to "Get Info, then choose "Sharing…" (below, left) to get the Sharing dialog box.

OR hold down the Control key and press on the folder. From the menu that pops up, choose "Get Info," then choose "Sharing…" (below, right) to get the Sharing dialog box.

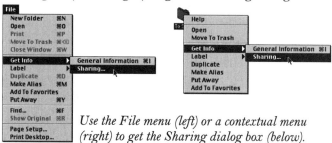

Use the File menu (left) or a contextual menu (right) to get the Sharing dialog box (below).

c. Click to put a ✓ in the box, "Share this item and its contents." You can change the privileges: the person at the other computer can "read only" (glasses icon; they can't make changes), "write only" (pencil icon; to make a folder so people can give you files), or they can have "read-write privileges" (glasses and pencil icon) where they can do anything.

Click the close box *or* press Command W to close the dialog box.

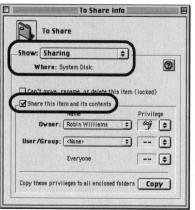

If this "Show" menu says "General Information," click on it to choose "Sharing." If it doesn't have the option "Sharing," the selected item cannot be shared. Maybe it's an alias? If so, find the original and then Get Info.

If you want the other person to be able to read these files and/or perhaps to make changes to the file, you can grant permission right here. Just check the boxes of your choice.

d. Now the folder will show wires coming out the side, as shown below. The wires are a good visual clue that this folder is willing to share. Anything you drop into this folder will be available to the person on the other Mac.

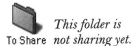 *This folder is not sharing yet.*

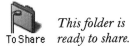 *This folder is ready to share.*

Rather than go through the steps manually, you can **let the Mac make a shared folder for you automatically:**

Make a shared folder automatically

Shared Folder

◆ Make sure no folder or disk icon is selected (click on the Desktop). From the Apple menu, slide down to "Automated Tasks" and choose "Share a Folder." If you didn't have one or more folders selected, the Mac will make one for you. It's automatically set up with read-write privileges for everyone. You can rename it.

You can, if you choose, **share your entire Macintosh.** Instead of choosing individual folders to share, choose your hard disk icon and share it (Steps 5a–5c). You must first make sure there are no existing shared folders on the hard disk (see below). You won't see wires coming out of your hard disk icon once it's sharable.

Share your entire hard disk

To find folders that are being shared, use Sherlock

a. From the Apple menu, choose "Sherlock."

b. Click on the first box, where it says "name." From the menu that drops down, choose "folder attribute."

c. The middle option box will change to "is." Leave it like that.

d. The option on the end probably says "empty." Press on it and choose "shared."

e. Click the "Find" button. Any folders that have been set up to share, whether they are actually being shared right now or not, will appear in the list. Right in this list, you can select the folder, get its Get Info window, and turn off the sharing.

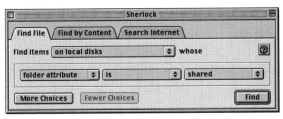

You might be surprised at the folders you find that you forgot you shared!

STEP 6:
Set up Guest
Access

You don't have to do this step—you can skip it altogether. If you *don't* do this step, then to share your computer a person has to know the correct name and password to connect to your machine; with that name and password they will have access to your entire hard disk.

If you *do* follow this step, you can arrange it so a person does not need a password—they can log in as a "guest," and they will only have access to the specific folders you give them privileges to.

To provide access as a guest

Users & Groups

a. On **Mac A,** from the Apple menu, open the control panel "Users & Groups." It looks like this:

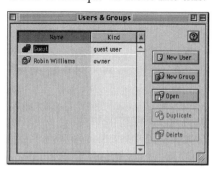

b. Double-click the name "Guest." You'll get this dialog box:

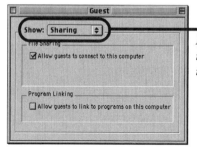

If the "Sharing" option isn't showing here, choose it from this menu.

c. The "Show" menu in this dialog box probably says, "Identity." Click on it and choose "Sharing," as shown above.

d. Check the box "Allow guests to connect to this computer."

e. Click the close box, then click the Users & Groups control panel close box also.

Continue on to the next step. You can always come back here and add new users, give entire groups certain access, and more. If you know that much about networking, you'll know what to do with the other options here.

Now the *other* Macintosh, **Mac B** (the iBook, probably) needs to connect to the bigger Macintosh, Mac A. Once you do this, you won't need to do it again unless the file-serving Mac (Mac A) turns off the sharing. After you set this up the first time, make an alias of your server icon so you can just double-click to connect to the server (see page 110).

To actually connect to the other computer, you can use either the Network Browser or the Chooser; both are in the Apple menu.

To connect to the bigger Mac using the Network Browser

Note: The file-serving Mac (Mac A) must be turned on and have file sharing on.

a. On **Mac B** (probably the iBook), open the Network Browser from the Apple menu.

b. You should see the name of the file-serving Mac (Mac A, here named "Robin's Hard Disk"). Click on the little triangle.

c. You'll get one of the dialog boxes shown far below. If you followed Step 6 to set up a Guest, that option is available. If Mac B logs on as a Guest, the Network Browser displays the folder you set to share (shown bottom, left). If Mac B logs on as a Registered User, the Network Browser displays the entire hard disk (far below, right).

A Guest does not need a password, but access is limited to the individual items that were set up to share on Mac A.

d. Double-click the shared item you want access to. An icon will appear on the Desktop of Mac B (the iBook, if that's how you've been following the steps) and its window will open automatically. It can be confusing—watch the folder names! Go to Step 8.

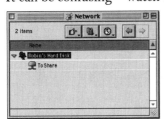

STEP 7:
Connect the Other Mac to Yours

Using the Network Browser (instead of the Chooser)

Network Browser

If you set up to share the entire hard disk, then even a Guest will have access to the entire hard disk.

To Share   Robin's Hard Disk

The icons for a shared folder or a shared disk look the same.

Using the Chooser
(instead of the
Network Browser)

To connect using the Chooser

Note: The file-serving Mac (Mac A) must be turned on and have file sharing on.

a. On **Mac B** (the iBook) from the Apple menu, open the Chooser (shown below).

b. Click the "AppleShare" icon. (If you were on a big network with "zones," you would see all the zones listed here also.)

c. You should see the name of the file-serving Mac (Mac A, here named "Robin's Hard Disk") on the right. Click on that name.

d. If you followed Step 1, the AppleTalk button is already on. You cannot share files without it.

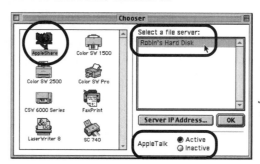

AppleShare

This is the AppleShare icon that must be in your Extensions folder.

The AppleShare icon is critical. You must have the AppleShare file in the Extensions folder in your System Folder.

e. Click OK. This will give you one of the dialog boxes shown below:

If you followed Step 6 to set up a **Guest** *user, the Guest button will be available and the user does not need to know a password.*

If you did not follow Step 6 to set up a Guest user, the Guest button will not be available. The **Registered User** *must know the correct name and password, including capitalization and spaces.*

You can change the password here, but you need to know the original password to do so.

f. Click "Connect." This will give you one of the dialog boxes shown below. Click the names to select the folders or disks you want to share.

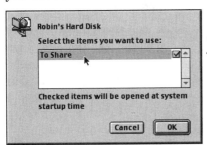

*If you logged on as a **Guest,** you will see only the specific folders that were set up to share in Step 5.*

*If you logged on as a **Registered User,** you will have access to the entire hard disk. In this example, each of the individual partitions of my hard disk are available.*

*Be sure to **highlight** the name of the disk you want access to—the checkmark does something else!! The **highlighted** disk is the one that will be shared for you—the **checkmarked** disk will be opened next time you turn on **Mac B.***

If you check "Save My Name and Password," you won't have to enter those next time you log on.

g. The checked items, as the note in the dialog box says, will be opened and shared every time you turn on Mac B. They will only open and share at startup on Mac B **if** Mac A was turned on first and **if** file sharing is activated on both computers!

h. Click OK in this sharing dialog box, and the Chooser will again appear in front of you. *Don't click OK on the Chooser or it will think you want to connect to the server again!* Instead, click in the close box in the upper left of the dialog box.

i. On the Desktop of **Mac B** (the iBook) you should see an icon like this for each folder or disk you have chosen to share:

The icons for a shared folder or a shared disk look the same.

STEP 8:
***Now* You Can
Share Files!**

To Share

On **Mac B** (the iBook), double-click on this "file serving icon," which represents the folder on the file-sharing Mac A, and it opens to a window just like any other folder. Anything you put in this "folder" will be **copied** to Mac A.

To Share

On **Mac A,** the shared folder icon changes when Mac B (the iBook) has successfully connected (a visual clue). Can you believe how cute this is—happy little people sharing files? Any file you drag from Mac A to this folder will **move** into this folder, and then the person on Mac B (the iBook) can drag that file out of their "To Share" folder, and it will be **copied** onto their Desktop on Mac B.

If Mac B (the iBook) has access to the entire hard disk of Mac A, the hard disk window from Mac A will appear on the Desktop of Mac B. You can drag any files from any Mac A folder onto the hard disk of Mac B, and you can drag any files from Mac B into the hard disk window for Mac A and the files will copy over. It's really amazing.

***Twitching while
file-sharing***

While the computers are file-sharing, you'll notice they go through little spasms and twitches and your typing stops for a second or two, menu commands take longer to happen, and other little annoyances will irritate you because the computers are trying to do two things at once—the work you want, plus send a file.

***Where are those
shared files?***

Important—please read this!

Let's say I'm working on **Mac A** and I put a file into the shared folder so You on Mac B can use it. When I put the file into the folder on **Mac A** (the server), I am actually just *moving the original file* into the folder because I am on the file-server Mac **(Mac A).**

You, on **Mac B,** want to use that file. You double-click on your shared folder on **Mac B** and see the file. **Don't double-click on that file that's inside the folder!!** What *You* see in that shared folder is the original file that is still on *My* hard disk, Mac A, and if You open that file, *You will be using My computer!*

> **Instead:** Copy the file to your hard disk on **Mac B** and then open it! To copy the file, just drag it from the shared folder onto your hard disk window.

You, on **Mac B,** when you put files from your hard disk into the shared folder, you'll see that the computer **copies** the files from your hard disk on **Mac B** onto my hard disk on **Mac A.** This means that when I open my shared folder on **Mac A,** all of the files in it are already copied onto my machine. Thank you.

When either computer shuts down, file sharing is automatically **disconnected.** You can also disconnect yourself from the "network" in several other ways:

Disconnecting

This is the icon of the file server on Mac B.

- ◆ Drag the icon of the *file server* on **Mac B** to the trash. You will not see any icon of the file server in the trash can window, so you can't go get it to reconnect.

- ◆ **Or:** select the file server icon on **Mac B,** then press Command Y (the keyboard shortcut for "Put Away" from the File menu).

- ◆ **Or:** on the file-serving **Mac A,** go back to the File Sharing control panel and click the "Stop" button. **Or** choose "Stop File Sharing" from the Automated Tasks item in the Apple menu.

- ◆ You can selectively disconnect users on **Mac A** through the File Sharing control panel, the same one you used to start the connection process: Open the control panel, then click on the tab labeled "Activity Monitor" (shown below).

    Click once on the name of the connected user you want to disconnect, then click the "Disconnect" button. Notice you can also change the privileges of any shared items from here.

File Sharing

Also use this control panel to change privileges or disconnect users.

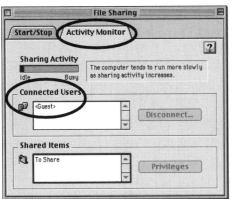

You will get a dialog box that says users will be disconnected in, for instance, 10 minutes. You can change that number to 0 (zero) and they will be disconnected immediately. They'll get a message on their screen telling them they have been disconnected.

If you need to turn off file sharing, do any one of the following:

- ◆ From the Apple menu, slide down to "Automated Tasks," and choose "Turn File Sharing Off."
- ◆ In the Control Strip, click the file sharing button and choose "Turn File Sharing Off."
- ◆ From the Apple menu, slide down to Control Panels, choose "File Sharing," and click the "Stop" button.

You can, of course, use any of these techniques to turn file sharing back on.

Turn Off File Sharing (or back on)

Reconnecting

To Share alias

Double-click the alias to automatically start file sharing without having to go through the Network Browser or the Chooser.

To reconnect Mac B (the iBook) to the file-sharing **Mac A,** you *can* go through the process of getting the Network Browser or the Chooser and logging on again, just like you did the first time. Or you can do one of these great tricks:

♦ In the Network Browser, select the icon of any of the folders or disks you want to connect to—drag the icon out of the Network Browser and drop it on the Desktop or into any folder. It will automatically make an alias for you (without the word "alias").

♦ If you used the Chooser, then when you *are* connected, make an alias of the file server icon on **Mac B** (the iBook) that represents the shared folder. To make the alias, click once on the icon, then press Command M.

Store this alias wherever you like. **When you need to connect to Mac A, just double-click the alias.** This trick will also work if you make an alias of some file in the shared folder.

First of all, the device called the **AirPort Base Station** (about $300, shown to the right) and the **AirPort Card** (about $100, page 113) are not *included* with your iBook, so if you don't have them, don't think Apple forgot to send them to you. We're telling you here what we know about this technology because it's so incredible and useful. Read the following and decide if it would be useful for *you* or not.

What the AirPort Base Station allows you to do is connect up to ten iBooks that have AirPort Cards installed (or other computers that are ready for wireless technology) to each other and to the Internet **without any cables at all.** Really. None. You can take your iBook up to the attic and cruise the Internet without being plugged into anything.

(You'll see ads showing people connecting while they sit by the pool or at an outdoor cafe, but notice you never see the screen in those ads—that's because you *can't* see the screen in broad daylight. We know this.)

Up to ten iBook users can transfer files, connect to the Internet, or play multi-player games within 150 feet of the AirPort Base Station (or an iBook that has been designated as the software access point, see the next page). Since the AirPort technology uses radio frequencies to communicate, it's not necessary to have an unobstructed line of sight between computers—the iBooks can be in separate rooms, inside, outside, or even a floor above or below another computer. Macintosh PowerBook laptops that have third-party wireless PC Cards (like the SkyLINE Wireless PC Card from Farallon) can also communicate with the AirPort wireless network. This is great for schools, offices, or even homes where the computer is replacing the television in kids' rooms.

An iBook with an AirPort Card installed sends the Base Station wireless signals. The Base Station passes them along to the network or Internet connection and sends signals back to the iBook, thus giving the little, unwired iBook the same access to network services as any of the other bigger, wired computers have.

With a cable you can **physically connect** an iMac or a Power Macintosh G3 to the Base Station, enabling *that* computer to also share the Base Station modem, share files, and play multi-player games with other computers connected to the AirPort's wireless network. Simply connect one end of a crossover Ethernet cable to the computer's Ethernet port, and connect the other end of the cable to the Base Station Ethernet port. Then set up your file sharing as explained in this chapter.

AirPort Base Station

Below you see the front and the back of an AirPort Base Station.

How does it work?

Add wired computers to the network

Access points

Wireless networking requires a bridge between the wireless network (like your iBook if it has an AirPort Card installed) and a wired network (like the Internet or a corporate network in an office or university). In wireless-network lingo, this bridge is called an **access point.**

- ♦ The AirPort Base Station is a **hardware access point,** which means it's a stand-alone device that creates an access point, or bridge, between a wireless and a wired network.

- ♦ An iBook with an AirPort Card installed can actually be used as a **software access point,** which means you don't have to buy the AirPort Base Station. This is a particularly useful option if you have a small office or several computers in your home that you want to connect wirelessly.

The AirPort Card's **Wireless Access Point Configuration Utility** enables you to designate an iBook as a software access point. And if you have an existing wired network, you can set things up so all of the other wireless-enabled computers will have access to that wired network through the iBook. Amazing.

The modem in the Base Station

The Base Station has a built-in 56K modem for connecting to the Internet. It also has an Ethernet port for connecting to a cable modem, a T1 line, or a DSL (Digital Subscriber Line). If you have a cable modem, T1 line, or DSL line, you'll enjoy significantly faster connection speeds than with a 56K modem.

The **AirPort Card** is a wireless LAN card (LAN stands for Local Area Network, which means all the computers on the network are in the same building). Once the AirPort Card is installed, your iBook can communicate with an AirPort Base Station, as described on pages 111–112, or with other computers that have wireless LAN cards installed.

AirPort Card

When you buy the AirPort Card, you'll have to install it. Read the directions. It goes under the keyboard.

Install the card

You'll install the AirPort Card in here.

You'll have to install the **software** that comes with the AirPort Card. Since the AirPort Cards and Base Stations are not available as we write this book, we can only tell you what we deciphered from the early documentation. As fas as we can tell, the software that comes with the AirPort Card has four components:

Install the software

- ♦ **Setup Assistant:** This utility walks you through the step-by-step procedure to set up a simple network.

- ♦ **Wireless Networks Application:** If you have more than one AirPort Base Station with computers connected in separate networks, this application allows you to switch between them— you can choose to have your iBook link into any one of the available wireless networks. This software also allows you to create and join **peer-to-peer networks**, also known as Ad Hoc Networking, which is direct communication between two wireless computers without using an access point. More simply, if you just want to network two or three iBooks at home, you don't need an AirPort Base Station—you could set up an ad hoc network.

- ♦ **Wireless Control Strip Module:** This is a control strip module you can add to your Control Strip that gives you access to all of the options in the Wireless Networks Application, above, with the added feature of a signal strength indicator.

♦ **Wireless Access Point Configuration Utility:** If you're an advanced user, use this utility to edit the administrative and advanced settings for hardware or software access points. You can also set up a software access point as a gateway to the Internet, or determine which location on a network has the best reception and will make the best access point.

Peer-to-peer networking Up to ten iBooks with AirPort Cards installed can communicate directly with each other. From the AirPort control strip module, you would choose "Direct computer-to-computer communications" (which is also called peer-to-peer or ad hoc networking) instead of "AirPort Hardware Access Point."

The AirPort control strip module Sometimes you'll want to connect your iBook to different networks at different times. You might connect to the office or school network during the day and to your simple home network at night or on weekends. The AirPort control strip module lets you switch between these networks.

The control strip module also allows you to turn off power to the AirPort Card when you aren't using it, which will help to maximize the battery life.

If you're traveling on an airplane, the airline may require you to turn the AirPort Card off, just as they do other radio signal devices. The control strip makes this a quick and easy process.

How secure is AirPort wireless communicaion? AirPort wireless communication is as secure and private as it would be on a normal wired network. You must enter a password to log on to an AirPort network. And, if you like, you can require a password to allow access to any other computer connected to the AirPort network. When the AirPort is sending information, it uses something called 40-bit encryption to scramble data, which is decoded when you receive it.

Part II. Email

In this section we look at the email programs that are installed on your iBook so you can make a choice about which one you would prefer to use. We talk about multiple email accounts that make it easier to pick up your email while you're traveling around the world, a little bit about email etiquette, and how to find a connection just about anywhere.

Email Options

This chapter discusses the software packages already installed on your iBook that you can use to send and receive email: Outlook Express, Netscape Navigator, and America Online. EarthLink is also on your iBook—you can get set up with an email account *through* EarthLink, but you'll need to use either Netscape or Outlook Express to read and send email.

As we discussed in Chapter 4, to send and receive email you need two things: an **Internet connection** through an Internet service provider (ISP) plus an **email program** (sometimes called an email client).

When things go wrong with your email, contact your ISP.

- ◆ If you use **America Online** to connect to the Internet, that is your ISP (Internet service provider) and your email client all rolled into one. You can have up to five individual names with individual passwords with one account.

- ◆ If you get yourself set up with an **EarthLink** account, they are your ISP and they will give you an email address. You can use Netscape as your browser and email client and the EarthLink web site to check your mail.

- ◆ If you use a **local ISP,** you can usually arrange for more than one email box and password with one account. You can use **Outlook Express** or **Netscape Communicator** as an email client.

- ◆ If you use a local ISP and Microsoft **Internet Explorer** as your browser, Internet Explorer will open Outlook Express as your email program to check your mail.

- ◆ If you have a **school account** or **corporate account,** ask your network administrator how to check your email outside of the school or office! The following chapter will also give you some tips on how to do this.

All Email Applications

The email applications on your iBook have certain things in common:

♦ **More than one person** can use the same account, but every person has their own private email with their own private password (except EarthLink—they charge you for extra email addresses).

♦ An **address book** so you can keep track of people and their email addresses (and all their other contact information), and you can enter email addresses with the click of a button instead of typing the whole name in.

♦ You can make an **email list** so you can mail the same message to a number of people with one click of a button.

♦ You can **file incoming email** into different files or folders for organizational purposes.

♦ **Write email offline** (when you're *not* connected to the Internet), then log on (connect) and send them all with the click of a button.

♦ If you're interrupted in the middle of writing a letter, you can save your document. When you are ready to continue it, open the letter, finish, and send.

Set the Default Email Application

Mail

The Mail icon opens the default email application.

Internet Explorer 4.5

Internet Explorer uses the default email application, even if it's America Online.

Netscape Navigator

Just FYI: Netscape **Communicator** *is a suite of applications.* **Navigator** *is just the browser; it uses the default email application.*

As discussed in Chapter 4, you can use the Internet control panel to choose a default email program (shown below). This affects the "Mail" icon and the browsers Internet Explorer and Netscape *Navigator* (which you probably don't have—you have Netscape *Communicator,* which uses its own email client). If you have installed your own email application that you want to use, choose "Select…" from the menu of options (circled below) to set it as the default.

In the Internet control panel (choose "Internet" from the Control Panels list in the Apple menu), choose a default email client.

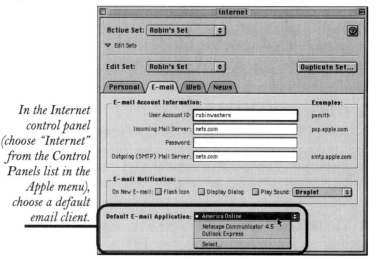

America Online (AOL) is a great introduction to email and the Internet. It's easy, there are guides to help you, there are rules against bad behavior, and there are clubs and chat rooms in which to make friends.

You can have up to five different "screen names," which are also your email addresses. Each screen name can have its own password, so five different members of your family can each have private email on the same AOL account.

Once you've made new screen names, you can choose which name to log on with.

To make new screen names or delete old ones, log on and go to the "My AOL" button in the toolbar; choose "Screen Names."

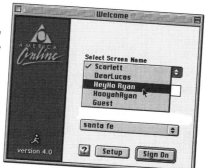

Each screen name can have its own "buddy list," a popular little accessory that shows a list of your friends all over the Internet (not just on AOL). When any of those friends are online anywhere in the world, their name appears on your monitor and you can send them an "instant message." An instant message shows up on their computer in a little message box, and it's private—no one sees it but the person sitting at that computer.

This is a Buddy List. You make the list, and if that person is online, their name appears in this window. An asterisk means they just appeared, and a name in parentheses means they have logged off.

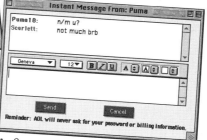

This is an Instant Message. Notice Scarlett and her friend are using "baudy language," online typing shortcuts.

Translation: *Puma: Not much. You? Scarlett: Not much. Be right back.*

Experiment! The best way to learn how to use America Online and to learn about all the features it offers is to **poke around.** Check out everything in the menus and everything in the toolbar across the top. Most things are pretty obvious: To read your mail, click the "Read" icon (if you have mail waiting for you, a little letter will be sticking out of the mailbox). To write a new email message, click the "Write" button. To add an attachment to a message, like to send a photo, click the "Attachments" tab on the email form, then find the file you want to send.

Double-click any letter in the list to read it. The icon to the left of the message changes to give you clues as to whether it's unread, read, includes an attachment, etc.

Click the other tabs (Old Mail, Sent Mail) to see those letters.

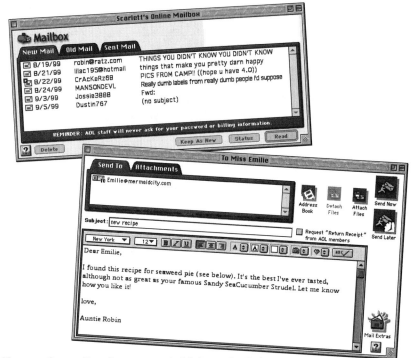

*Shortcut for sending the message: hold down the fn key and tap **Return** (the fn key changes your iBook's Return key into an Enter key). If you're not using an iBook, just hit the Enter key to send the message.*

The first thing people seem to figure out in AOL is how to make an email list of everyone they know so they can send everybody junk mail. Please don't put us on your list.

To create an address book entry

1. From the "Mail Center" menu in the toolbar, choose "Address Book," or click on an Address Book icon wherever you see it.

2. Click the "New Person" icon and fill in the information. Click OK.

To create an email mailing list

1. Add the names of all the people you want in your address book (per above), regardless of which list you will put them in later.

2. Click the button "New Group," name it, and click OK (yes, I know there are no names in it yet).

3. Press on any name in the list, drag it to the group name, and drop it right on the group name. The address will be *copied* into the group list.

To address an email message from the address book

♦ Open a new message, click the "Address Book" icon, and double-click the name of a person or group to whom you want to send the message.

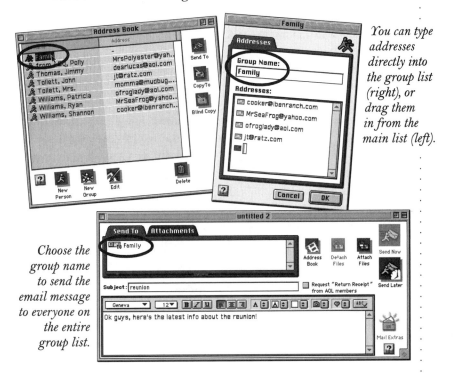

You can type addresses directly into the group list (right), or drag them in from the main list (left).

Choose the group name to send the email message to everyone on the entire group list.

Use the Personal Filing Cabinet — AOL has a Personal Filing Cabinet for each screen name that you can customize with your own organized folders. You can then choose to save your mail into specific folders, and you can access them offline.

To create and use folders in the Personal Filing Cabinet

1. From the Mail Center menu in the toolbar, choose "Incoming/ Saved Mail." You'll get a box like this:

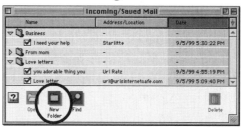

2. Click the "New Folder" button to make a new folder; name it. Make other folders, if you like. Click the close box (upper-left corner) to put this box away.

3. Check your mail as usual. If you find a letter you want to file into one of the folders you made, open the letter.

4. While the email letter is open, go to the File menu (above the toolbar) and choose "Save to Incoming Mail Drawer" (shown to the left). You'll see a hierarchical menu off to the right side, with a list of the folders you made earlier. Choose the folder you want to save the open letter into.

5. Open your Personal Filing Cabinet whether you're online or offline: from the AOL toolbar menu called "My Files," choose "Personal Filing Cabinet." You won't see your folders yet. First click the tiny arrow next to "Offline Mail." Then click the arrow next to "Incoming/Saved Mail."

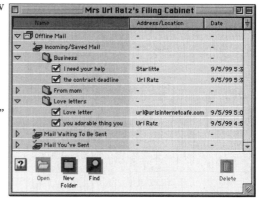

6. Use the "Passwords" section in "Preferences" if you want to set a password for your filing cabinet.

You can make new folders directly in the Personal Filing Cabinet, but they won't show up in the File menu when you save them. If you want new folders to save directly into, repeat Step 1.

It's very easy to send a photograph to someone else with an America Online account. You want to make sure the photograph is in the format called JPEG because if it's not, it will take a long time to send through the phone lines. How do you know if it's a JPEG? Most photographs have the three- or four-letter extension, either .jpg or .jpeg, at the end of the file name that gives you a clue. When you get your own photos developed, ask the service if they can put them on a CD for you in the JPEG format; many places can do this now. Almost any photo you find online is in the JPEG format, so if it's already on your screen, it's most assuredly a JPEG photo. If you have a friend who knows graphics, ask them to help you scan your photos and save them as JPEGs.

The biggest problem with JPEG photos is that the same features that make it a good choice for online viewing make it bad for printing—most photos that look great on the web don't look so great when you print them.

To put a photo in an email form to send

1. The easiest thing to do is first find the JPEG file on your iBook.

2. Then open an email form in America Online (you don't have to be connected).

3. Drag the JPEG over to the email form and drop it in the message area.

4. Send the message. If the person receiving the message also uses America Online, it's guaranteed that the photo will look great when it gets to their machine. If the person receiving the photo does not use AOL, the photo might or might not come through just fine—it depends on the kind of computer and email client they use.

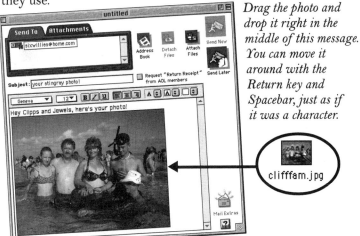

Drag the photo and drop it right in the middle of this message. You can move it around with the Return key and Spacebar, just as if it was a character.

PictureViewer

Don't forget about the QuickTime PictureViewer, as we discussed on page 66. When you get any sort of graphic image attached to your email, you can drop its icon on top of this icon and the image will display. The PictureViewer is in the QuickTime folder, which is in the Applications folder.

Send a photo

Netscape Communicator and Messenger

Yes, Netscape Communicator is a browser, but the version of Netscape called Communicator (as opposed to the version called Navigator) includes a great email client: Netscape Messenger. The first time you open Netscape Communicator, it asks for information with which to make a "user profile" for you. This information includes your email specifications. If you look in the Preferences file (from the Edit menu), you'll find everything you entered in the profile there in Preferences. Once it's in Preferences (and you can change it there, if you like), Messenger picks up the information so it can get your mail.

Click one of these, or press Command 2 to get Netscape Messenger.

To access Messenger, just click once on the tiny inbox icon at the bottom right of the browser window, or if you see the floating palette, click on the "Inbox" button or word (as shown to the left). This will bring up Messenger. You'll be asked for your password, and then your mail will appear in a window like this:

Whether you see icons or text in this toolbar depends on what you choose in Preferences, in the "Appearance" section.

The inbox

Click one of these options to see the messages stored in that folder—the list will then appear in the top-right box. Right now, "Inbox" is chosen, which displays the incoming mail.

Click a message to display it in the box below.

Double-click a message to open it in its own window.

Message in bold means it's unread.

While a message is displayed, click the "Reply" button at the top to open a new email message form addressed to this person, with a copy of their message in the form.

Click here to return to the browser.

To resize each panel, *drag on the borders between them. To resize the entire window, drag the bottom-right corner of the window.*

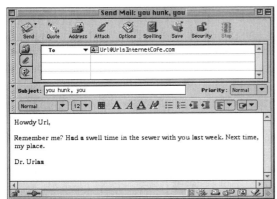

When you click the "New Msg" button, you get a nice form like this. Use all the fancy bold, italic, indent, numbered, etc., buttons only if you know the person on the receiving end uses either the same email client or one that can read that kind of information. You might have to experiment.

Make a new message

You can rearrange the look of your email window. Drag on the circled bars. The folders that were on the side will now be in the pulldown menu directly above "Subject." When you double-click on a message, it will open in its own window.

Reshape the inbox window

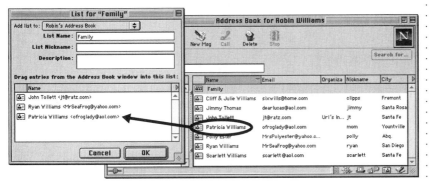

Make an address book and mailing list

To make an address book, *go to the "Communicator" menu at the top of the screen and choose "Address Book." Click "New Card" in the toolbar and enter the information in the box that appears. Click* OK.

To make a mailing list, *first make your list of addresses. Then click "New List" in the toolbar and name it. Click* OK, *then drag the names from the address book into the mailing list box (shown above).*

To mail to the entire mailing list, *go to the address book.* **Press** *on the mailing list name in the right panel and hold the mouse button down—you'll get a menu (shown, right). Choose "New Message."*

Preferences　The best thing to do to learn Messenger is to check out all the menus, especially including the Preferences (from the Edit menu). Here are a couple of things you should look at carefully.

If many of your options for changing informa-tion are grayed out, Messenger may be picking up information from something called Internet Config. In Netscape, go to this preference ("Identity" in the "Mail & Newsgroups" section) and uncheck the box, "Use Internet Config."

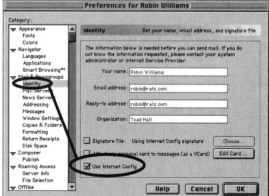

Check out all the preferences for the mail program.

The font and size in which you read messages is whatever you chose in the "Fonts" section (under "Appearance" at the top of this list) for the "non-proportional font."

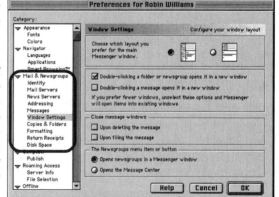

If you are on a network in a large office and you want to be able to check your email at someone else's computer in the office, fill out the information under "Roaming Access," including "Server Info" and "File Selection."

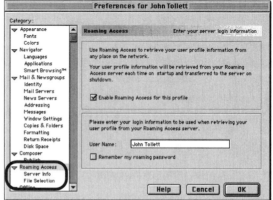

Netscape Communicator lets you make multiple "user profiles." This allows more than one person to use the same browser, but each person can set their own preferences and check their own email. The profiles themselves are not password protected, so anyone can open anyone else's profile; you still need a password to check the email, though.

Make profiles for other users

Once you have made at least two profiles, Netscape will always open to the list of profiles so you can choose one.

To make a new user profile in Netscape Communicator

1. Quit Netscape if it's open.
2. Find and open the folder for Netscape Communicator. If you don't know where it is, look in the "Internet" folder, then look in the "Internet Applications" folder to find the "Netscape Communicator Folder."
3. Find the file called "User Profile Manager" (shown to the right). Double-click it.
4. Click the "New" button and fill in the information requested.

User Profile Manager

The easiest way to find this might be to use Sherlock Find File.

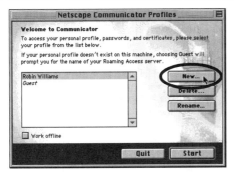

5. Once you have more than one profile stored, you will always get the dialog box to choose a profile, and you'll always have the button available called "Manage Profiles" so you can make new ones, delete unnecessary ones, and rename others.

Outlook Express

Outlook Express

Microsoft Outlook Express is an email client that, as you'll notice, looks and acts very much like Netscape Messenger. If you use the browser Microsoft Internet Explorer and have set Outlook Express as the default email application (which it is if you haven't changed it; see page 87), then when you click an email link on a web page or click the Mail button in the toolbar (circled, below), Explorer will open Outlook Express for you.

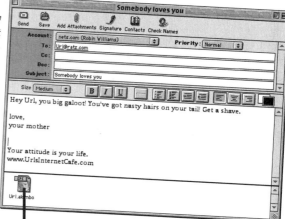

Choose "New Message" in Internet Explorer or choose "New" in Outlook Express to get a blank message form. It's pretty self-explanatory.

This is an attached file. Click the "Add Attachments" button in the toolbar; this leads to a dialog box where you can find the attachment on your computer and send it along with the message.

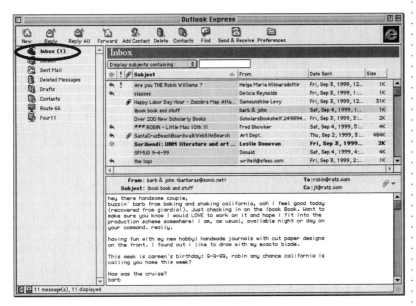

The basic Inbox

Click once on a message and it will display below.

Bold messages are unread.

Symbols to the left of the messages indicate whether they are read, unread, replied to, or have attachments. The exclamation point indicates high priority (according to the person who sent it).

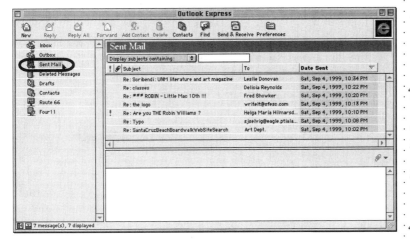

Like all email clients, Outlook Express keeps track of the mail you sent in case you need to refer back to it.

"Deleted Messages" are not really thrown into the Mac trash can—they are put in a deleted file in the email client. This means you can look at them again when necessary. To really get rid of them, open the folder called "Deleted Messages," then go to the Edit menu and choose "Empty Deleted Messages." (This is true of all email clients, not just Outlook Express.)

*Make an address
book (Contacts) and
a mailing list*

You can make an address book, called "Contacts" in Outlook Express, and you can make a mailing list so you can mail a number of people at once (but please see the etiquette rules on page 134).

To make a contact list

1. Open Outlook Express.
2. Either click the "Contacts" icon in the toolbar, or press Command 2.
3. In the Contacts window, click the "New" button in the toolbar and enter the information.

To make a mailing list

1. Make a contact list first (you don't *have* to, but you might as well because then you have the option of sending email individually or to the whole group). See above.
2. Click the "Mailing List" icon in the toolbar, and name the list. Click OK.
3. Drag the names from the Contact list (on the right) and drop them on the Mailing List name (on the left), as shown below. Copies of the addresses will be added to the Mailing List— the addresses will remain in the Contacts list as well for sending individual emails.

*Drag a
contact name
to a mailing
list name to
add a copy of
that address
to the list.*

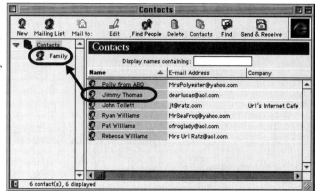

To mail to the entire mailing list

1. Open the Contacts window.
2. Click the name of the mailing list you want to send a message to.
3. Click the "Mail to" button in the toolbar. This opens a new message addressed to the mailing list group.
4. **Or** open a new message. Open the Contacts window. Drag the mailing list group icon to the message window.

Most Internet service providers allow you several email boxes with one account so your family members can each have their own individual, password-protected mailbox. Or you might like to have more than one inbox yourself—one for business, one for personal, and one for family, for instance. You can set up Outlook Express to check the email for each account.

Make accounts for other users

To set up multiple user accounts

1. First talk to your service provider and arrange the extra email accounts. They will give you the information you'll need to set up the user account in Outlook Express: the SMTP server, the account ID, the address, the password, the POP account information, the NNTP server if you want access to newsgroups, etc. Don't worry about what it all means—just write it down.

2. Open Outlook Express.

3. From the Edit menu, choose "Preferences...."

4. In the Preferences dialog box, click the button for a "New Account...."

5. Fill in the blanks. Check the other preference settings and adjust them to fit the new account. Click OK.

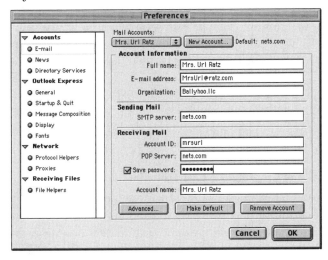

To switch to the new account while Outlook Express is open, go to the File menu and choose "Change Current User...."

Signatures

Every email client lets you attach an automatic **signature** to an email message (well, in America Online it's not *automatic*). A signature is any message you type that you want to appear at the end of your email. You may have seen them on other email letters before. A signature might include your name, phone number, fax number, web site address, and perhaps a quote. Or some people make fancy little "ASCII" (askee) pictures out of typed characters.

To make a signature in Netscape Messenger

1. First, find and open SimpleText. Write the message you want to appear as your signature, and save the file with a simple name.

2. In Netscape, open Preferences (from the Edit menu). Click the "Identity" choice under "Mail & Newsgroups."

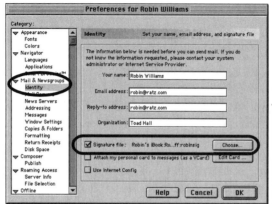

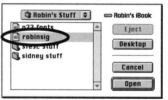

Either click the "Signature file" checkbox or click "Choose…" to get the dialog box where you can find your signature file.

3. Check the box for "Signature file." This will automatically open the dialog box where you can go find the file you just made.

4. Select the signature file, then click "Open." The text you wrote in that file will appear in all of your new email messages.

To make and use a signature in America Online

♦ AOL doesn't have automatic signatures. They suggest you type the text into a file, then when you want to use that text as a signature, open the file, copy the text, close the file, open your email message, and paste the text at the end of it. Here's a slightly simpler solution:

Type the signature test in an email message, or into the AOL notepad, in SimpleText, or in the Mac Note Pad. Select the text, drag it to the Desktop, and let go. This makes a "text clipping." Rename the clipping. To put this signature into any email message, drag the clipping from the Desktop and drop it into the email form.

urls sig

This is a text clipping (renamed). Drag it into any email form.

To make and use signatures in Outlook Express

1. Open Outlook Express.

2. From the Tools menu, choose "Signatures...."

3. In the "Signatures" dialog box, click the button at the top called "New Signature."

4. In the "Edit Signature" dialog box, type your signature. In an email message, you'll be able to tell it to choose from a random list of signatures. If you want this particular sig in the random list, click the checkbox. Click OK.

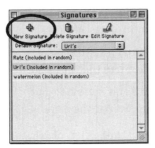
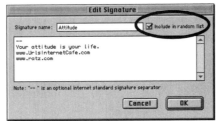

5. Make more signatures, if you like. From the little "Default Signature" menu in the dialog box (above, left), choose the one you want as the default (automatic) choice.

6. In the email form, choose one of the signatures from the "Signature" button in the toolbar. Choose "Random" to let Outlook Express choose one from the list.

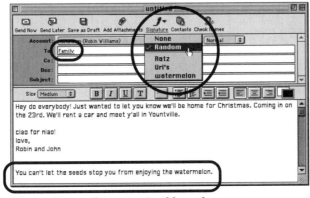

Notice this email message is addressed to the entire Family group.

Email Etiquette   Please, follow a few polite guidelines with email.

♦ Don't type messages in all capital letters. Besides being more difficult to read, all caps is the equivalent of SHOUTING.

♦ Don't forward chain letters to anyone except those you *know* would be happy to see one. That does not include us.

♦ Don't forward your junk mail (like joke lists or sentimental stories or Internet legends) to anyone except those you *know* would be happy to see it. That does not include us.

♦ If you do forward junk mail (which is anything except your personal mail), please do this:

> **Select** the text of the mail, the important stuff. **Copy** it. **Paste** that text into a **new** message. **Send** that message.

This eliminates the incredibly boring and annoying list of email addresses that collects at the top of the page.

♦ If you send a message to your entire mailing list, please send it in the BCC (blind carbon copy) slot (every email client has this feature). This prevents your entire mailing list from appearing on the mail and saves friendships—many people don't want their email address broadcast to the world in this form. Sent as a BCC, every person on the list thinks they are the only person who received this message.

♦ If your friends send you well-meaning but annoying junk mail, refer them to **www.UrlsInternetCafe.com/classroom/junkmail**. It will give them the message and if their feelings get hurt, you can blame it on Url.

♦ If you send an attachment to someone, state in the email message what kind of attachment it is, how big it is, how it was compressed, what kind of computer you made it on (Mac or Windows), etc.

♦ Don't send a large attachment unless you *know* the person will be happy to see it.

Url Ratz demonstrating his technique for filing junk mail.

Portable Email Accounts

Now that you have an iBook and you're no longer confined to your home or office to use your computer, you'll start looking for ways to make your computer-mobility even easier and more efficient.

Receiving email is usually not a problem when you're at home or at the office, but how will you pick up your mail if you're traveling out of your area—or out of the country—without incurring costly long-distance charges?

You might have an email acount where you work that serves you perfectly well at the office and at home. But if you change jobs, chances are slim that the network administrator is going to let you keep your old email address, topdog@acme.com.

Or, if you're a university student, you might have a student account that allows you to retrieve email from any web browser on any computer, but what will you do after you graduate or after you leave school early to start your own Internet-based business?

Many people have more than one email address. You might have one for work, one for home, and one for lovers only. Or you might have an email address on your web site so customers can request information, and another address for family and friends. You might, like John, have a free email web account so you can check all of your email from all accounts at one place, or like Robin, have a secret address that only a select few people know (and she hardly ever checks that one either).

National Service Provider

One solution to being able to pick up your email anywhere in the country is to have an **Internet service provider** (ISP) that offers **nationwide** connectivity. Many companies offer affordable plans that allow Internet access through their huge national networks or through special arrangements with affiliated ISPs around the world (a feature known as "global roaming"). Typically a plan like this will make local access numbers available to you in major cities. Or, if you find yourself in a small village with one telephone, the ISP plan will usually provide an 800 number that provides access to a regional ISP at a reasonable rate.

Here are the names of a couple of the most popular national service providers:

EarthLink (continental US)   **www.earthlink.com**
Well, EarthLink also provides service to places like Alaska and Hawaii, but it costs $9 an hour. They can also provide international access at a much higher price.

MindSpring   **www.mindspring.net**
(formerly Netcom and SpryNet)
MindSpring is a partner of GRIC, the major international service. Having bought Netcom and SpryNet, MindSpring now has more local dial-up numbers all over the world than any other provider. This is your best choice if you want an international ISP.

For a more complete and regularly updated list, check Yahoo **(www. yahoo.com);** click down through the Yahoo directory—click **Computers,** then **Internet,** then **Commercial Services,** then **Access Providers,** then either **National (U.S.)** or **International.** The lists you'll see are links to providers.

Get a Local Account

If you plan to be based somewhere else in the country for a month or more and your current ISP doesn't provide an access number for that area, sign up a new account with a local ISP. For a contact list of many thousands of Internet service providers around the country and the world, go to **www.thelist.com.**

Another way to collect email anywhere in the world is to sign up for a free email account on the Internet. Free-mail accounts are available from many places online (see the partial list in the side column). Because you can access this kind of account anywhere in the world, you can keep the same email address even if you change jobs, switch ISPs, or move.

To sign up for a free-mail account, go to one of the web sites, fill out the online form, and assign yourself a user identification name and a password. Almost immediately you'll have your new email account and you'll be able to send and receive email using any web browser. It's really quite amazing.

(A free email account is not an ISP! You must have some sort of Internet connection or at least access to a connection, like at a friend's house or work or at an Internet cafe so you can use a free-mail account.)

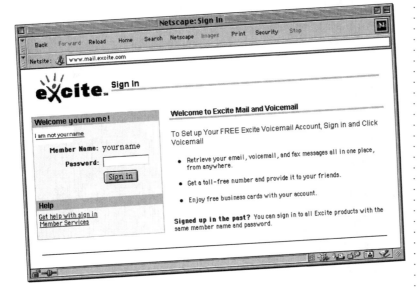

If your free-mail site offers something called "POP Mail" or "POP3," you can also check any other email accounts you may have with other ISPs or at your office. "POP3" stands for "Post Office Protocol" and refers to incoming mail. When you log in to the free-mail provider's site, you should find a link called something like "POP Mail." Click on that POP link to go to a form (shown on the following page) where you can enter the server address (mail server), user ID, and password for any other email account you may have. Once you've submitted this form, checking

Web-based Free Email Accounts

The following sites offer free email. Some offer custom addresses, like doctor.com or biker.com. For a comprehensive list of free email sites, go to **www.emailaddresses.com.** It's a phenomenal site full of great information, including customer reviews of various services.

AltaVista	altavista.iname.com
Netscape	webmail.netscape.com
Excite	mail.excite.com
(voicemail, fax, and more)	
AmEx	amexmail.com
PO Box	pobox.com
NetAddress	usa.net
Yahoo	mail.yahoo.com
My Own Mail	myownmail.com
ProntoMail	prontomail.com
RocketMail	rocketmail.com
MailCity	mailcity.com
iName	iname.com
MailStart	mailstart.com

Check all of your email accounts from one place

all of your other email accounts from your free-mail web site is as simple as clicking the POP link after you've logged into your free-mail account.

The "Mail Server" or server address is something you might need to ask your ISP or account manager for, if you don't know exactly what it is. The user ID and password on the server are not necessarily (and probably not) the same as your email address name and password! The ID and password the POP form wants is the internal information your ISP uses. You might need to call them and ask what it is.

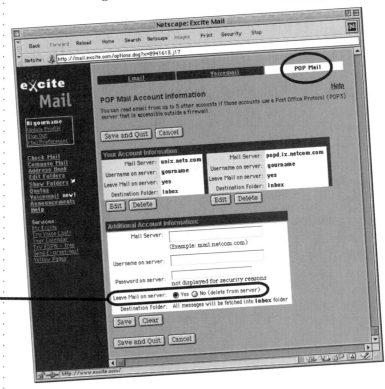

The POP form will allow you to designate whether or not to delete email from a server after downloading it to your computer. See page 140 for an explanation of this.

Use POP to Retrieve Company Email

Now, the process above includes being able to check your office email from a remote location. For instance, if you work in a corporation with a large intranet (private network), your email is on the corporate server and you can't dial into it. You can create a POP3 account on this free-mail web page so you can check your office email from anywhere in the world. Talk to your system administrator to get the required information (server address, user identification, and password). If the intranet is behind a firewall (security protection), talk to your system administrator to see if it's possible to get permission to get your mail through the firewall.

Check any existing email account on the web at **www.thatweb.com.** This is an incredible site. Just go to their page, type in your email address and your password, and it will go get your email. You don't have to sign up, fill out any POP preferences, nothing. It's free. There are several of these kinds of sites, but this is our favorite. They can't check AOL accounts, though. See the note below if you use AOL.

This site, thatweb.com, doesn't delete the mail from the server (see the following page for clarification on deleting mail from a server) so you will still have access to any mail you read on thatweb when you get back home.

Many Internet cafes (as mentioned below) and many friends' computers have AOL software installed. If it's installed, you can log on as "Guest" from any computer, enter your own password, and check your mail. If there's any billing, it goes to your account, not your friend's. But as you travel you might run across computers that either don't have the AOL software, or if you are connecting with your iBook, you might not find a local number for AOL. So sign up with AOLNet, which allows you to check your AOL mail from a web page. As long as the computer has Internet access and a good browser, you can get your AOL mail anywhere in the world. Go to **www.aol.com/netmail** and sign up. When traveling, go to the same address to check your email.

As you travel, even to foreign countries, you'll find a growing number of communities that have **Internet cafes.** Some of these cafes may have data ports that you can plug your iBook into, but most cafes won't. In this case, it's very convenient to have a free email account that you can access from the cafe's computer. It won't be as much fun as using your iBook, but it'll work.

For a list of the Internet cafes around the world, check the web site at **www.netcafeguide.com.** You'll be amazed at the unlikely places in the world that are connected. You can search by country or city or any place name. This site offers a handy little book for sale, *Internet Cafe Guide*, by Ernst Larsen, that you can take with you on your travels that lists 2,300 Internet cafes in 113 countries.

If you don't have a place to connect your computer and there's not an Internet cafe available, try the local **public library.** Many libraries have computers connected to the Internet that you can use to log in to your free email account.

Check Any Existing Email Account

Check AOL Mail with or without AOL Software

Internet Cafes

Public Libraries

Save Your Email   When someone sends you email, the letter doesn't just float aimlessly in the outer limits waiting to be found by you when you're online. The email is sent to the server (a special computer) whose name is referred to in your email address; for instance, if your email address is **joe@ hotdog.com,** the name of your server is usually (not always) **hotdog.com.** When you check your email, the computer dials the number of the server where you have an email account and looks in your mailbox *on that server* to see if you have any mail that hasn't been delivered to you. If there's mail, the server usually copies it to the hard disk of *your* computer and then generally *removes* it from its own server. (America Online keeps your mail on its huge server for thirty days, then deletes it; that's why your email stays in your mailbox for a while, even after you've read it, then magically disappears.)

Now, it's important to understand that (unless you're using AOL) your email might be instantly deleted from the server after it's downloaded to a hard disk. This means **if you check your email on a foreign computer, your mail might now be on** *that* **computer and you won't have access to it when you get back to** *your* **home or office computer.** Different free-mail web sites have their systems set up differently, so until you experiment, you can't be sure your email will be accessible when you get home or not.

To solve this potential problem, you can do several things. One, if the foreign computer lets you change the preferences, uncheck the button that says something like, "Delete mail from server." This ensures that when you get back to your own computer, the email you read while away will still be available to you. (See the note and illustration regarding this on page 138.)

Another thing you can do if you read mail on another computer but want to make sure you don't lose it, is to simply forward the mail to yourself or to another account that you won't check until you get home. You could even set up a new free-mail account specifically for forwarded messages that you will retrieve later.

Part III
On the Road

One of the greatest things about the iBook is, of course, its portability. Since the Internet and email are such important parts of our lives, we often want to connect everywhere we go. The iBook has several special features just for this desire.

It's pretty easy to connect just about anywhere in America, but a few accessories will come in very handy. And when you leave the country, there are things you must know and accessories you *must* buy before you go if you want to connect successfully overseas.

Before You Leave Home

You can connect from anywhere. You can use a cell phone, a pay phone, a hotel digital phone, you can go through a PBX switchboard, an airplane phone, the satellite on a cruise ship, or an old rotary phone in some quaint backwoods motel. You can connect anywhere in the world, even if there is no visible port in which to plug a modem.

You *can* do it, but it's not always easy. The trick is to be prepared before you leave home. You might need accessories, adapters, converters, couplers, or other odd pieces. You might need to adjust your software to accommodate foreign phone systems. Don't be like us—we ran off to Paris totally unprepared with our laptop and modem with plans to update our web site for friends and family back home. It didn't work. We learned a lot.

In this chapter we explain about all the accoutrements you might need, and in the next chapter we tell you how to actually use them.

We can't tell you *everything* you'll need to know, but we can get you started and give you resources for where to find exactly the information you need for connecting in any country in the world. This is too much fun.

How Important Is It?

For some people, connecting is fun but not critical. For others, it's very important. And then you have those obsessed people (like Robin and John): it's fun, it's important, and we just want to prove we can do it!

For those of you in the strictly fun category, the following information may not interest you. But if you're determined to optimize your connection odds, we've got some tips for you.

We've discovered that when traveling and mobile-computing with a laptop, preparation works much better than optimism. For instance, let's say you're taking a short weekend trip. Since you're not leaving the United States, you assume that your hotel room's phone will be compatible with your iBook's modem. But when you get there you discover that the hotel has a digital phone system. This discovery may take the form of a blown-out modem, as happened to a friend of ours. And, just trust us on this one, you won't be able to get a new modem from room service.

You will have fewer problems connecting from the States than trying to connect from a foreign country, but being prepared for a worst-case scenario will not only make your connection attempts successful, it'll add a road warrior swagger to your walk. If connecting is important while you're away, carry a couple of extra gadgets with you and go through this checklist before you leave.

Help for Mobile Connecting

Mobile connectivity can be challenging. We don't have all the answers, but we know someone who does. TeleAdapt **(www.teleadapt.com)** offers knowledge, expertise, and a fantastic range of products, accessories, and connectivity solutions. Besides adapters, converters, and gadgets, TeleAdapt also has 24-hour global tech support packages that can be purchased for 3, 6, or 12-month durations to fit your travel needs. And there's no limit to the number of calls.

TeleAdapt can make even your most unusual modem connection attempts successful. You may never have thought of connecting to the Internet from a phone booth, but that was before you knew it was possible.

You might also want to check out **www.igo.com.** They also specialize in mobile connectivity, although their focus is strongly on Windows machines. The iGo company has lots of accessories and gadgets for people on the move, besides for connectivity.

Does your hotel use a digital phone system? Call ahead and find out, or take along a digital converter just in case. But the hotel clerk may not know if the phones are digital, or there may be a language barrier. If you have an IBM Modem Saver (shown below) or some other type of line tester, you can determine if the line is safe to use.

You stick the IBM Modem Saver into any standard RJ-11 wall jack. If the wall jack is not accessible, disconnect the phone cable from the telephone. Snap an RJ-11 coupler (shown below) onto the end of the cable, then insert the Modem Saver into the coupler. The status lights on the Modem Saver indicate dangerous line conditions, such as an **overcurrent,** or "reverse polarity" (see the following page). An overcurrent is an indication of a digital line, requiring a digital converter such as the TeleSwitch Plus (shown below). The TeleSwitch Plus converts dangerous digital signals to recognizable and safe analog signals.

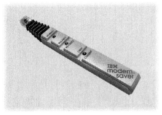

This IBM Modem Saver is about as big as a writing pen and costs about $30.

This little coupler, available in any office supply store, costs about $5. Always carry one or two of these with you.

This TeleSwitch Plus digital converter fits in your hand and costs about $140.

Use the data port

If you're in a fancy hotel, it most likely has a digital phone line through its PBX switchboard. Don't plug your modem into the phone or the wall! You'll blow out your modem. If you see a jack on the side or back of the phone, or sometimes built right into a desk, labeled "Data" or "Data Port," plug your modem into that jack. The data port is specifically designed for analog modems, which is what is built into your iBook (and just about every other computer).

Beware
Reverse Polarity

That line tester we mentioned on the previous page can also tell you if the phone jack is wired incorrectly (for a modem), called **reverse polarity.** If it is, having a tiny little device called a Polarity Reverser can be a lifesaver. When connecting once on a ship, we had an IBM Modem Saver that told us the line's polarity was reversed, but we didn't have the small, affordable Polarity Reverser that would have solved the problem. Reverse polarity won't harm your modem, but you probably won't be able to connect.

This Polarity Reverser fits in your hand and costs about $15.

Do You Have
Enough Cable?

Do you have an RJ-11 **cable** (phone cable) long enough to plug in o the phone and place your laptop where you'll be comfortable? A retractable RJ-11 cable is very handy, especially if you're in a cramped and crowded location, such as an airline seat where a long cable could be a nuisance.

A retractable cable costs about $15.

It would be much easier to use a laptop in first class. Sigh.

These are
Always Useful

Before you leave home, always throw in a couple of RJ-11 **couplers** and **doublers.** You might need a coupler to "couple" two cables together for a longer cord, or to connect a line tester to a cable. You might need a doubler to connect both your iBook and the phone to the wall jack, or to connect your modem and a pocket phone to the telephone when you need to manually dial. It's amazing how often these little things come in handy.

This is a coupler. It costs around $5.

This is a doubler. It costs around $5.

Some digital telephones do not support auto-dialing (that's when your modem or fax software automatically dials a number); they insist on hearing the touchtones from the phone itself. In that case, you'll need to **manually dial** the number using the telephone touchpad.

To determine if the hotel switchboard you need to get through will let your modem auto-dial, pick up the phone handset, get a dial tone, and press some of the buttons. If you don't hear any touchtones, the system does *not* support auto-dialing and you'll have to manually dial.

For a situation like this, you should carry an **RJ-11 doubler jack** (shown to the right) to make sure you can connect both the phone and your modem at the same time (instead of having to unplug the phone so you can plug your computer modem into the jack).

You might also want to have on hand a **pocket phone** for those times when you find a wall jack but no telephone, yet you need to talk to an operator to get your connection through. Along with your pocket phone, of course, it would be a good idea to have a doubler and a coupler just in case.

This is a handy pocket phone. It costs around $20.

If you think you might be in a situation where you desperately need to connect and the only thing available is a **pay phone,** well then you had better have an acoustic coupler along with you. No data port to plug into? No problem. Just use the Velcro strap to attach the coupler to the pay phone handset and connect the acoustic coupler cable to your iBook. This will work with almost any type of phone, including digital PBX systems and hard-wired phones without any sort of modular phone jack connections.

This is an acoustic coupler. You'd be surprised how often it comes in handy when you're traveling. It costs around $130.

Will you Need to Manually Dial for your Modem?

Doublers are always useful.

Pocket Phone

Pay Phones

Surge Protector Power surges in the electrical lines can send damaging currents through your computer. A **surge protector** can save you a lot of grief, not to mention your iBook. Just the peace of mind you get with a surge protector is worth the price.

For iBooks and other laptops, these devices aren't the big, clunky power-strips from yesteryear—they're small and sleek, weigh a few ounces, and can easily be thrown in your travel bag. They look pretty cool, too. You may even want to have a couple of them with you because a power surge strong enough to blow out the portable surge protector can render it useless and you may need to replace it with another.

This is one type of surge protector (on the left, $20). It plugs into your power adapter, that box in the middle of your power cord.

The iBook has what's called a "C5/C6 connector," also known as a "cloverleaf," which is quite common, but just make sure your surge protector is compatible.

Local Access Numbers
all over the country

If you and your iBook plan to travel around the country, connecting along the way, you should have access to an ISP that offers **nationwide local access numbers.** EarthLink and MindSpring are two such ISPs, as well as AOL. Be aware that even though EarthLink calls itself a "national" ISP, residents of Alaska and Hawaii have to pay international phone rates instead of a flat monthly fee, and it's $9 per hour.

If you plan to travel internationally, MindSpring is your best choice (see page 136). They have partnerships with ISPs all over the world and can get you connected just about anywhere.

Calling Cards A telephone **calling card** or a prepaid phone card is a giant help when your situation requires long-distance access, whether it's from another office, a friend's house, a hotel, or a phone booth. The Dial Assist control panel can be set up to automatically dial access numbers, personal identification numbers (PINs), country access codes, and more. See Chapter 9 for details on using Dial Assist and setting up different connection configurations with Remote Access.

If you plan to call internationally, make sure you get a phone card or calling card with international access. And be sure to get the access codes before you leave home! See Chapter 11 for details on connecting internationally.

If you travel to the same places regularly, like from home to office or from school to parents' house, use the **Location Manager** control panel to create customized configurations that make it easy to change computer settings for different locations. These settings are not just for connecting, but for a variety of different settings you might need. *If the Location Manager confuses you, skip it! You can live forever without this!*

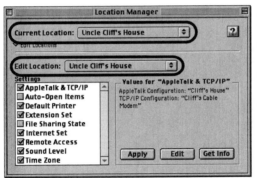

*Notice that this upper menu lists the **current location**. The lower menu is for editing. You can choose two different locations in these two different menus, so if you want to **choose** a new location, be sure to use the upper menu, not the lower, editing menu.*

The Location Manager control panel (shown above) displays the various settings you can customize. Within each "module" you see listed on the left, you can set up your preferences. There are two ways to do this.

♦ In one location, such as home, make sure everything is set up the way you want it on your iBook. Don't use the Location Manager to do this—just go to each of the areas you see in the Settings list above and set them. With AppleTalk, TCP/IP, and Remote Access, you won't be allowed to save a configuration that is named "Default," so you must make a new configuration before you go to the Location Manager (if you want to customize those settings); see the explanation on the following page on how to make a new configuration.

Then when everything is customized the way you like it, open the Location Manager (from the Apple menu, slide down to Control Panels and choose "Location Manager" from the list). From the File menu, choose "New Location...." You'll be asked to name it, so do. When you click OK, all of the checkboxes in the Location Manger will be unchecked. Just check the ones you modified, and you're done. When you close the control panel, you'll be asked if you want to save the changes. Click "Yes."

When you get to your next location, open the Location Manager. Make a new location, as above, and edit each of the settings of your choice.

Use the Location Manager

The Location Manager is also useful if two or more people share one iBook. Each person can set up their preferences, and then start up the iBook with them.

Make a new location

AppleTalk *is a communications bridge between the Mac and other devices, like certain printers, other computers, through Ethernet cables, or through a wireless connection.*

TCP/IP *is the protocol that tells your Internet connection and email messages where to go and how to get there.*

Remote Access *tells your iBook which number to dial to connect, plus has some other techie specifications for your modem. For details of Remote Access, see Chapter 4 and check the index.*

♦ The other way to make a location is to go straight to the Location Manager control panel, make a new location (from the File menu), and edit the existing settings. As mentioned previously, you can't edit AppleTalk, TCP/IP, or Remote Access from the Location Manager unless you have first created at least one configuration other than "Default" (see opposite).

Choose a location Once you have made more than one location, you can tell the iBook to
on startup give you the choice on startup of which location to use.

To make the iBook ask you which location to use

1. Open the Location Manager control panel.

2. From the Edit menu, choose "Preferences...."

3. In the settings for "Startup Switching," choose one of the options.

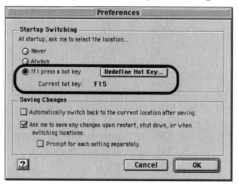

If you click the radio button "If I press a hot key," the button "Redefine Hot Key..." becomes active. A "hot key" is a key you press when the iBook is starting up that forces the iBook to give you a choice of locations to startup with, shown below.

You can be content with the default hot key, which is the Control key, or you can click the button and type the key you want to use.

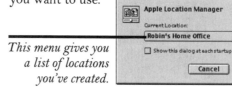

This menu gives you a list of locations you've created.

♦ In the Preferences dialog box, if you check "Ask me to save any changes...," then when you make changes to any of the settings that the Location Manager keeps track of, you will be asked if you want those changes applied to the location.

It can be confusing when the Location Manager yells at you about AppleTalk (or TCP/IP or Remote Access) having "Default" settings because if you go to those control panels and make changes to anything, they still look the same and the Location Manager still yells at you. What you need to do is make a new **configuration** named anything except "Default."

Make a new configuration for AppleTalk, TCP/IP, or Remote Access

This is the "Default" the Location Manager is fussing about.

To make a new configuration

1. Open the control panel in question (AppleTalk, TCP/IP, or Remote Access).

2. From the File menu, choose "Configurations...." In each of the three control panels, you'll get this same dialog box:

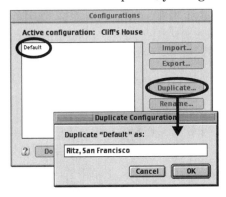

If the Location Manager seems like it might be useful to you, get all the juicy details in the Help file. Open the Location Manager, then from the Help menu, choose "Apple Location Manager Help."

3. This is confusing because now in this dialog box there is no button to make a new anything! Do this: Click once on "Default" to select it, then click the "Duplicate..." button. You'll be asked to name this duplicate configuration. Name it and click OK. You now have your same settings, *but it's not named "Default."*

4. Close the control panel. You'll be asked if you want to save the changes, and click "Save." Now you can go on with your Location Manager editing.

Please see Chapter 11 for details on connecting abroad.

International Travel

If you're traveling **internationally,** try to use an ISP that offers a global roaming option, such as GRICtraveler, available through MindSpring Enterprises, Inc. **(www.mindspring.com).** MindSpring has joined the GRIC Network Alliance, which has thousands of local access numbers of member ISPs from around the globe. These phone numbers are available to MindSpring subscribers in their downloadable software, GRICdial. MindSpring will soon have its own branded version of the GRICdial software.

If you're going to use GRICdial software to connect to "local" ISPs while traveling out of the country, go online before you leave and update the software's Phonebook to the current active phone numbers. Simply double-click the GRICdial application to open it, then press on the "File" menu and slide down to "Update Phonebook." If you haven't already established an Internet connection, GRICdial will dial your ISP, connect to the GRICtraveler database, and update your phonebook. These numbers can't be edited manually in your software, they have to be updated through the web site. GRICtraveler will even connect users to company intranets via a secure VPN (Virtual Private Network) connection.

International Power Plugs

If you're an international traveler, find out in advance what kind of **power adapters and telephone sockets** you'll need in your destination country. There are hundreds of different wall sockets around the world and dozens of differently shaped telephone jacks.

The iBook's power adapter can handle power supplies from 100 volts to 240 volts AC (50 Hz to 60 Hz), which eliminates the need for a voltage transformer. This ensures that the power adapter you have will work in most areas of the world *IF* you have the correct adapter to plug into a foreign wall socket.

TeleAdapt **(www.teleadapt.com)** has power adapters and telephone adapters for 260 countries, including Regional Power Packs that contain collections of adapters for entire continents, with multiple adapters for countries that have a variety of power plug standards.

iGo.com also has a great collection of international mobile computing tools and accessories.

Connecting on the Road

Be sure to read the previous chapter about preparing your iBook before you leave home, because this chapter puts into actual use all the products we displayed and discussed in Chapter 8. You might also want to make sure to read Chapter 6 about the advantages of different email accounts, especially if you're traveling. And if you haven't already set up the iBook so you can make a connection to the Internet, be sure to read Chapter 4.

In this chapter you'll travel cross-country with Url Ratz, proprietor of Url's Internet Cafe.com and self-anointed Internet Icon. Along the way you'll experience various conditions to challenge your Road Warrior prowess, and you'll pick up some useful tips, too. After you've been on the road with Url, you'll be ready for many challenging connectivity situations that you might not have thought were possible to overcome.

Why Travel with your iBook?

Even though this chapter is all about connecting as you travel, we recognize that while Internet connections and email are reason enough to carry the iBook with you, they aren't the only reasons. Even if you don't want to check your email or your favorite web sites, it's still great to have the iBook along. You can get a lot of work done, using the software that's bundled with the iBook or with any software you've installed yourself. You can play music CDs or interactive game CDs. You can draw, paint, read, write, calculate, schedule, or rescue Lady Bugs from Fire Ants (Bugdom) without ever connecting to the Internet. So rest assured you'll have plenty to do between connection sessions.

Now let's make sure that when you want to connect away from home, you'll be able to.

To demonstrate the various challenges and solutions that you may encounter with mobile connectivity, we're going to send you on a road trip with our associate, Url Ratz, and the two of you will connect from different places. You'll be sharing an iBook, so try to get along.

The Trip

Url's plan is to leave from Url's Internet Cafe World Headquarters in Santa Fe and drive to New York City, meet his pal, Browser, then fly from New York to San Francisco where he's scheduled to be the keynote speaker at the Macworld Exposition.

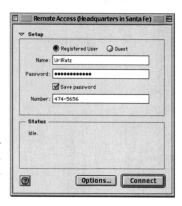

Planning Ahead

Url has an ISP account with MindSpring, an international provider, so he'll have plenty of local access numbers to connect through as you travel across the country.

At home, Url had already created a setup configuration in the Remote Access control panel that contained his name, password, and the local access phone number for his ISP.

This is Url's basic configuration for connecting at home. He chooses this configuration from the Remote Access control strip when he wants to connect.

Because Url plans to drive as far as Amarillo the first night, he checks MindSpring's web site **(www. mindspring.com)** to see if Mind-Spring has a local access number in Amarillo that he can use when he gets there. From the MindSpring home page, Url clicks on "Access Numbers" which links to a database of local access numbers listed by state.

Great, there is one. Url sets up a new Remote Access configuration and names it "Amarillo TX." Now when he gets to Amarillo, he can just go to the control strip, click the Remote Access button, and choose the Amarillo setup.

Url can now choose which phone number to connect with, depending on where he is.

Hey, now's a good time for *you* to create other new configurations for cities you expect to be traveling through. You'll find complete directions for using Remote Access on pages 90–91. Simply put, you need to open the Remote Access control panel, go to the File menu and choose "New Configuration," make a duplicate of an existing configuration (you'll find one called "Default"), rename it, and make changes to it. That's it. When you close Remote Access, you'll be asked if you want to save the changes to this new one, and you click "Save."

(Because Url is using MindSpring, he doesn't need to make a new configuration in the TCP/IP control panel to match. If he had decided to use a local provider in Texas, he would have had to call them, set up an account, and plug all the DNS numbers and other data into not only a new Remote Access configuration, but into a new TCP/IP configuration as well, then choose both new configs when in Texas.)

The alternative to using MindSpring is to pay for a long-distance call to connect through his local ISP back in Santa Fe.

If you are an AOL user, you don't need to use Remote Access. Instead, open AOL as usual, then before you log on, click the "Setup" button. Click the choice, "Setup AOL to sign on from a new location…." Name the new location (such as "Amarillo"), choose the phone numbers, and click "Done." You'll have a new choice in the "Select Location" menu, as shown to the right.

In the hotel room

In the Amarillo hotel room, you're just about to connect the iBook to the phone jack when Url freaks and screams, "Stop! What if that's a digital phone system?" Url happens to have a **line tester** that alerts you to the presence of a digital line which would damage the iBook's modem (or any computer's modem). After you insert the line tester into the wall's RJ-11 phone jack (which is the standard sort of phone jack we're accustomed to), the indicator lights confirm Url's suspicions that it is indeed a digital line. Fortunately, Url always packs a **digital converter** that safely converts digital signals to analog signals.

This $30 line tester and the $150 digital converter prevented the destruction of the modem that would have happened had Url plugged his iBook phone cable into the hotel's digital phone system.

***Getting through
the hotel switchboard***

Thinking out loud, Url says, "If the PBX switchboard at this hotel only accepts **touchtone** signals straight from this telephone touchpad, we won't be able to connect using the software's usual autodialing feature. We'll have to manually dial the local access number." You ask, "How do we know if the system here supports autodialing?" Url says, "Pick up the phone's handset. When you get a dial tone, press several buttons. If you don't hear any tones, the system doesn't support autodialing." When you test the line you hear the touchtones. That's good, but you have a funny feeling that before this trip is over, you'll have a chance to "Dial Manually."

"Don't you need to dial 9 for an outside line?" Url asks. "Oops. Almost forgot, Url," you respond as you open **DialAssist** from the "Control Panels" menu and select a prefix to be automatically dialed. "Yo, Url! This DailAssist control panel lets you choose all kinds of information that will be dialed automatically by the software." "Yeah, duh," says Url.

Use **DialAssist** to tell your modem to dial country codes, long distance access numbers, prefixes (such as the codes for accessing outside lines), and suffixes (such as credit card or calling card PINs).

Using DialAssist

♦ In the **City/Area Code** field, type the area code *from which you are calling at the moment.* (You really can't type an actual city name in this field.)

♦ From the **Country** menu, select the country *you're calling from.*

Below are the boxes you get when you click the "Prefix..." and the "Long Distance..." buttons.

♦ In DialAssist, the **prefix** is a number you have to call before you call the actual phone number you want. For instance, the 9 you dial to get out of a hotel or office building is a prefix.

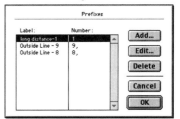

Select a prefix from the menu, if one is required from where you're calling. To add or edit a prefix, click the "Prefix..." button in the bottom section of DialAssist.

♦ The **long distance access** number is either the 1 you usually have to dial before a long-distance number **OR** the calling card, credit card, or prepaid phone card 800 number if you're not dialing direct.

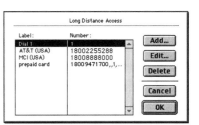

You should take a moment to enter all of your calling card, credit card, or prepaid phone card access numbers now: click the "Long Distance..." button at the bottom of the DialAssist control panel. If you plan to leave the country, make sure you get the long distance codes from your international access provider before you leave—it's a different number from the one you use in the States!

If, in the process of calling your card number, you have to wait for an automatic operator to tell you to do the next step or perhaps choose a menu selection (such as, "Press 1 to use your calling card), you must enter commas to force the dialing process to pause long enough for the operator to do her stuff. Each comma will pause the process for two seconds. Before you attempt to enter the number here in this dialog box, first get a pen and paper and make the call using the card. Write down all the pauses and the numbers you may have to push to get all the way through. For the *prefix*, you want all the numbers *up to the point* where you actually enter the long distance phone number you're trying to reach. For a calling card or credit card, this will be the access number and perhaps a menu choice; for most prepaid

Your long distance number might look like this:
18002255288,,1,,,

phone cards, the prefix will *include* your PIN number because the very *last* thing you dial is the number you want to reach.

So, enter your card numbers, then make a selection from the Long Distance Access menu.

Below is the box you get when you click "Suffixes...."

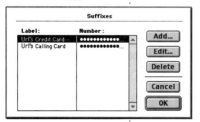

♦ The **suffix** is the number you have to dial *after* you dial the actual number you're trying to reach. For instance, if you use a calling card or credit card, typically you have to dial your PIN number *after* you dial the phone number you want. This PIN would be the suffix.

If you're using a prepaid phone card and you've already entered your PIN in the prefix, you don't have any suffix.

So, enter your suffix numbers, then choose the one you want at the moment from the Suffix menu. If none, choose "None."

♦ Click the close box in the DialAssist title bar.

♦ **To force your modem to use the DialAssist numbers** you selected, open the Remote Access control panel. If you don't see the checkbox for "Use DialAssist," then go to the Edit menu and choose "User Mode...." Click "Advanced," then click OK. Put a check in the box for "Use DialAssist." Notice the "Preview" shows you the number the modem will dial. The comma

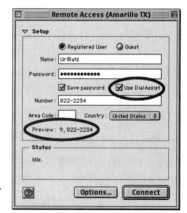

after the 9 will create a two-second pause to give time for the outside line to connect.

In this example, Url is not using a calling card—he's connecting to the local access number that MindSpring offers, but he has to get an outside line. In such a simple case, Url has an alternative to using DialAssist: he could type the 9 and the comma directly into the "Number" field here in Remote Access.

Okay, so once all the Remote Access and DialAssist (if necessary) fields are filled out appropriately, **make the connection:**

1. Open the control strip at the bottom of the screen.

2. Click the Remote Access module (the telephone pole and monitor icon) and select the "Amarillo TX" configuration.

Notice you can also call up the Remote Access control panel right from this menu.

3. Then click again on the Remote Access module and select "Connect." You should hear your modem squeal and you'll be online in a few seconds. Open your browser and off you go.

As you surf the Internet, Url says, "I'm expecting a fax. Browser said he'd send me a map of how to get to his house." Url opens his email software (Outlook Express). The fax that was sent to his free eFax.com account is in his Inbox attached to an email message. "When I'm on the road, I give friends my eFax number, along with my free voicemail number and my free email address. That way I can pick up all manner of messages from my browser and email programs."

For details on how to get (and use) free fax and voicemail services while you're on the road or staying at home, see Chapter 10; for free and portable email accounts, see Chapter 7.

Back at the ranch . . . I mean hotel

This is the tab for the control strip. It's usually in the bottom-left corner of your screen, although you can hold down the Option key and drag it up or down or to either side.

Pick up a fax online

Url views his eFax, left, through the free viewer that came with his free eFax account.

Use an Internet cafe

For information about Internet cafes, see page 139 in Chapter 7.

Your next stop is Eureka Springs, Arkansas. You've checked the MindSpring web site for the availability of a MindSpring local access number, but no luck. You could use a MindSpring 800 number and pay a reasonable fee per hour, but there's an **Internet cafe** in town and Url offers to pay for the coffee.

While you're at the Internet Cafe, Url suggests you get your own dang free email and voicemail account. You decide this is a really good idea since you need to email relatives to tell them you're on a road trip with a rodent. Many web sites offer these free services, but you choose to surf over to **excite.com** and spend five minutes setting up a new, free email account (see Chapter 7 for details of creating your own free email accounts, and Chapter 10 for voicemail accounts).

Check your other email accounts while on the road

You would like to also **check your existing email account** that you have with a local ISP back in your hometown, so Url shows you how to use your new Excite account (above) to check any other email accounts (called POP mail) you may have. See Chapter 7 for details of how to check your other POP email accounts from the free email web page.

Use an 800 access number to connect

Late the next night you don't even know where you are when you check into a dumpy, ratty (sorry) motel. You're not worried about the presence of a digital phone system so you go ahead and connect your iBook to the phone line. Having anticipated that this road trip could lead to some places where MindSpring would not have a local access number, Url had set up a Remote Access configuration that contained a **Mind-Spring 800 number** for Internet access. The 800 number access will have an hourly charge that MindSpring will add to Url's monthly ISP invoice, but the convenience is worth it.

Oh no, reverse polarity!

This $15 device can get you connected even if the phone is wired wrong ("wrong" according to a modem).

For some reason, the connection doesn't work. Url unplugs the RJ-11 phone cable from the base of the phone, attaches a coupler to the phone cable, and inserts his line tester. It indicates that the wiring in the phone jack may have **reverse polarity,** which means the wires are crossed and the modem can't connect properly. "No problem," Url says as he pulls a small polarity reverser out of his bag, hooks it up, and connects on through. Of course, he used DialAssist to add the MindSpring 800 number.

To connect the line tester (left) directly to the phone cable, Url used a handy coupler (right) he bought at the office supply store.

Printing & Faxing on the Road

This short chapter explains your limited options for printing while on the road, and summarizes using the FAXstf software that is already installed on your iBook for faxing when you are away from home. We also give you a few tips on receiving faxes from anywhere, through your email account. And there's even a tip about free voicemail you can check on a web page.

Printing on the Road

Frankly, you don't have a lot of options for printing on the road. We'll tell you all the options we know at the moment, but we expect the options for iBook owners will increase as vendors realize how many of these little machines are wandering around the world.

Portable Printers

As we write this (late 1999), there is only one **portable printer** for the Mac, the HP DeskJet 340, and it uses a serial connection; your iBook uses a USB connection, so you can't plug into the printer. But you *can* buy an adapter, such as the AccelePort USB-to-Serial (about $160). You plug this adapter into the iBook, and then plug the serial cable from the printer into the adapter. Because this particular printer is actually a Windows printer adapted for the Mac, we don't guarantee this as a perfect solution. But if you desperately need a portable printer, it's your only option today. We hope and believe this will change.

Hotel offices, or fax it to yourself

If you are in an expensive hotel, there is usually a **business office** with printers and **fax machines** especially set up for guests. Some hotel rooms include certain office equipment, such as a fax machine that will also receive your email, two-line phones, etc. While it's unlikely you'll be able to successfully connect to a hotel office printer (because they're usually set up for Windows machines), you can at least fax pages to yourself. If the fax machine is in your room, you've got instant hard copy. If the fax machine is in the hotel office, you can go collect it.

Use a service bureau

Every large city has **service bureaus** that take files from graphic designers and print them up on really expensive, slick film ready for the press. But they can also print to standard laser printers on regular paper for much less. It's possible you could take your file to a service bureau or email it to them, then go down later that day or the next day and pick up your hard copy. Look in the phone book under "service bureaus," "typesetting," "advertising," or "graphic design." Call them up first and explain what you need because they need to talk to you about the software you used to create your document, as well as the fonts you used.

Find the local Mac User Group

Most towns have a **Mac User Group,** a wonderful resource of Macintosh users who love to help people. If you're really desperate, call the local MUG and see if anyone can accommodate your printing needs. Remember that if someone does come to your rescue, they are doing it out of the goodness of their heart and taking time out of their life to save you, so please be appropriately and overwhelmingly grateful.

To find the local MUG, call Apple at 800-538-9696 and choose option number 5. Unfortunately, Apple has changed the way they find the local group—instead of asking for a zip code, they figure out where you are calling from and tell you the local group according to where you are at the moment. This means you can't call up and find out the local user group for a town before you get there. But you can go to Apple's web site and find the contact person for every user group in the world: **www.apple.com/usergroups.**

Different software packages and different typefaces can make printing to any printer but your own a frustrating experience. The **Adobe Acrobat** software solves just that problem. A file created as a **PDF** (portable document format) holds all the formatting and all the fonts and can be read on any computer (including Windows machines) and printed to any printer.

Use PDF files

On your iBook you have the Acrobat *Reader,* which will *read* files that someone else already created as PDFs. If you want to make PDFs yourself, you need to buy the Acrobat software (if you have other Adobe products, such as Photoshop, Illustrator, PageMaker, or InDesign, you can usually export files as PDFs without buying extra software). If you think you'll either be printing to strange printers or sending files to other computers for printing, or even just for viewing on-screen in the original format and typefaces, you should look into investing in Adobe Acrobat, or at least see if your existing software can make PDFs.

Some large **copy centers** can print up your file for you. If you have a floppy drive or Zip drive attached to your iBook, take the file on a disk; if not, call the copy center and see if you can email it to them, or see if perhaps you can hook up your iBook to their printer.

Copy centers

Kinko's copy centers offer a wonderful service. Go to **www.kinkos.com** and learn how you can electronically send a print order to any Kinko's in the world. At their web site, click the "Online" icon for instructions. You can also search from their web site to find the nearest Kinko's shop.

Print at Kinko's around the world

A growing number of airports are installing enclosed, lockable cubicles set up with workstations, modems, printers, fax machines, T1 Internet connections, and more. These cubicle systems are called **Laptop Lanes.** If you have a USB cable with you and the printer in the cubicle is USB, it's just possible you could connect and print. If not, you could at least fax yourself some hard copy. See more details in Chapter 12.

Laptop Lane
www.laptoplane.com

Faxing on the Road

Your iBook has the fax software installed called **FAXstf,** as we explained in Chapter 2. Although we described how to use the features to fax from your iBook when you're not at home, we know you won't read it until you need it. So here is a checklist of details you need to cover before you try to fax away from home.

♦ **To send a fax,** you are not connecting to the Internet so you don't need to worry about local access numbers, local ISPs, or international providers. You won't open a connection at all— the fax software has all the dialing information built in and will go straight out to the phone line.

♦ If you plan to **fax long distance** from a hotel, airport, airplane, friend's house, etc., you'll need a calling card from a phone company, or a phone card from any grocery store or street vendor, or a credit card with all of its attendant numbers.

♦ If you plan to **fax from another country,** you need an international calling card or phone card and you need to find out the access number for the countries you'll be visiting. That is, the 1-800 number you use in America will not work in other countries (except possibly Canada). You really should find out the number before you go because it's not always easy to find out the access codes once you're there. Check the web site for your calling card, or call the number on the back of the card. Not all calling cards or phone cards can make international calls, so make sure you get one that does.

♦ If you travel to certain places regularly, like to a certain hotel, office, lover's apartment, school, parent's home, etc., use the FAXstf software to set up various **locations** for each place. As shown to the left, the location holds the settings for your calling card, phone card, outside line, etc. When you're ready to fax, you can just choose a location and all of that information is automatically applied.

The locations are used with a feature called **Smart Dialing.** Please see pages 46–48 for all the details about Smart Dialing and locations. Keep in mind that if you plan to use Smart Dialing, you need to make sure the fax numbers in the Phonebook are consistent: every one, even local fax numbers, needs an area code, and don't enter the 1 for long distance because it's included in the location settings.

♦ You don't have to use locations. You can, if you prefer, enter any prefixes and suffixes for calling cards, phone cards, or credit cards in the **Dialing Settings** and let the fax software use those. The problem with using the Dialing Settings is that any numbers you enter as the prefix and suffix are dialed with *every* fax number you ever call so you have to put them in and take them out according to where you are calling from. But if you only need these long numbers once in a while, the Dialing Settings might be preferable to making various locations. See pages 46–48 for details about entering the numbers appropriately.

♦ With most calling cards and credit cards you have to dial an access code (the 1-800 number), then you might have to choose a number from a menu, then you dial the fax number, and then you enter the PIN number. So with these cards it's clear what the prefix is (all of the numbers *before* the actual fax number) and what the suffix is (all of the numbers *after* the actual fax number). Those are the numbers you enter in the Dialing Settings or Location List in the Prefix and Suffix fields.

But with the prepaid phone cards you buy in the grocery store or from your next-door neighbor, you usually dial the access code, wait several seconds to listen to directions, then you dial your PIN number, then wait several seconds while they tell you how much time you have left and perhaps even a dang commercial, and *then* you dial the fax number. Well, all those numbers before the fax number could be considered a prefix and you could enter them in the prefix field in the location box if you're making one. **OR** you could do this:

Enter all of those numbers, plus all the *commas* you need so the fax software waits while the person gives the commercial, into the **Macro** field in the Dialing Settings (details for doing this are on page 43). The number will look something like this:

18002568444,,,,,,987654321,,,,

Then in the fax number you want to call, add the letter **M** in front of the fax number (you won't need a 1 in front of the fax number to call long distance with a card). Then just send the fax as usual—the **M** represents your entire phone card number, including pauses (the commas).

If you're using a Location and Smart Dialing, you can put the **M** right in the "Long Distance Prefix" field.

Tip: *Before you go to the trouble of trying to make the computer send the fax, make a quick telephone call yourself to the fax machine using all the necessary numbers to make sure all your information is correct. That way if you need to troubleshoot, at least you'll know the number is correct and actually reaches a fax machine.*

A comma makes the dialing pause for two seconds.

Gather the
necessary accessories

To send a fax (or connect to the Internet) while on the road, you'll probably run into a wide variety of telephones—digital, pay phones, PBX switchboard systems, airline satellite connections, etc. Before you leave home, read Chapter 8 to learn all about the extra devices you need for making a phone connection away from home. We recommend, at a bare minimum, that you take these items along (prices are approximate):

- **Phone jack doubler** (available in office supply stores, $5)
- **Phone cable coupler** (available in office supply stores, $5)

    The following items (as well as the items above) are available through **www.teleadapt.com** and **www.iGo.com**.

- **Portable surge protector,** which you should use at home anyway ($20)
- **Line tester** to test the phone lines to see if they are digital (which will blow up your modem) and if the polarity is reversed (which won't hurt your modem, but you probably won't connect) ($30)
- **Polarity reverser** in case the wires in the phone line are crossed ($15)
- **Digital converter** to connect to digital hotel and office phone systems or you'll destroy your modem ($140)
- If you plan to connect from pay phones, you'll need an **acoustic coupler** ($130). The acoustic coupler can be very handy because it will also work on digital phone systems so you wouldn't need a digital converter.

There are lots of other great tools you can take along, but these will get you through most situations in North America. If you're leaving the country, read Chapter 11 because you'll need several other items.

Fax from your
cell phone

Nokia cell phone:
model 5160 or 6160

Modem card:
3Com Hertz 3CXM556
(available at any computer
store; software is on CD
and is Mac-compatible)

Cable: NOK-6 from 3Com

Not. Well, not from your iBook, not yet. At the moment the special modems you need for **cell phones** need to be plugged into either a serial port or a PC slot, neither of which are on an iBook. When someone makes a USB cellular capable modem, we can use it.

It was very difficult finding out cell phone/modem information. Every place we called gave us completely different information. We did find a Nokia rep who actually uses a cell phone with a Macintosh PowerBook, so **if you have another Mac laptop that has a PC slot,** he says the recommendations we listed in the left column will work perfectly.

Do you need remote access to faxes? Would you like to be able to use your iBook to pick up a fax that was sent to you on the road? Would you like to send faxes to someone who is traveling? Would you like it to be free? You're in luck. **eFax.com** offers several different faxing plans, although the basic plan is free and it may be all you need.

It works like this: Go to eFax.com and register. You'll be given a piece of software called eFaxMac for viewing the faxes and a fax number for your client to use to send you a fax. Unfortunately, it's not a toll-free number, but then, your client was going to have to make a long-distance call to your regular fax number anyway, right? You will receive faxes as email attachments that you can open, read, and print in the viewer. Now you can collect your client's fax from your hotel room or on the airplane instead of waiting until you get home.

Free Faxing with eFax.com

Like the proliferation of free email accounts via web pages, free fax accounts are going to start appearing everywhere. Keep your eyes open.

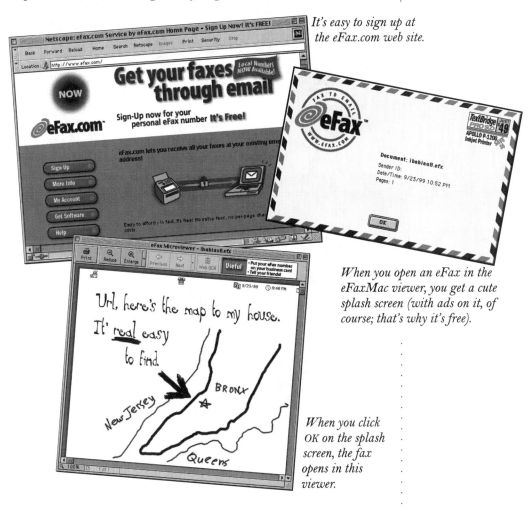

It's easy to sign up at the eFax.com web site.

When you open an eFax in the eFaxMac viewer, you get a cute splash screen (with ads on it, of course; that's why it's free).

When you click OK on the splash screen, the fax opens in this viewer.

Free Voicemail

Some of the same web sites that offer free email (see Chapter 7) also offer free voicemail. You'll get a toll-free number with a 10-digit access code (the 10-digit access code can be your home phone number) that you can give to friends, relatives, and business associates. Anyone can leave you a voicemail message up to 90 seconds in length. If you've signed up for a free Excite eMail account, any voicemail messages you've received will be noted in the same Inbox that contains your regular email.

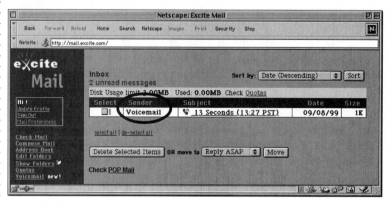

To listen to voicemail messages within your Excite account, you'll need the software called RealPlayer 5.0 or later. RealPlayer isn't included with the iBook, so you'll have to download it from the Internet. A lot of web sites have multimedia content that requires the RealPlayer, so it's nice to have even if you don't use voicemail. You can download RealPlayer at **www.real.com/products/player.**

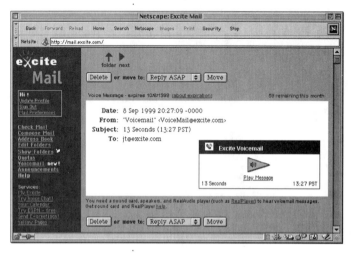

Click the voicemail link in the Inbox to display a window with a "Play Message" button. Make sure your speaker volume is loud enough, and click the "Play Message" button. RealPlayer will open and play the message. Amazing.

Excite voicemail only allows sixty voicemails per month. Don't complain—it's free.

Connecting from Foreign Countries

Connecting your iBook to the Internet from foreign countries involves some serious planning ahead. The power plugs are different, the telephone jacks are different, the dial tones are different, the calling card numbers you need are different, and more. And they're not consistently different; that is, foreign countries don't have *a* different telephone socket—there are about *forty* different ones.

As you read through this chapter, don't be overwhelmed and think it's impossible. Lots of people do it—you just can't go unprepared. You need to buy a few extra parts, and you need to get certain information for your software before you go.

Having unsuccessfully tried to connect from places like Paris and Rome, we would never again leave the country with a laptop without first consulting **TeleAdapt (www.teleadapt.com).** We're going to tell you the sorts of issues you need to deal with before you go, and TeleAdapt has all the products you'll need to connect in any country in the world, plus specific documentation for every kind of procedure you might have to go through. TeleAdapt also provides training and worldwide technical support. We couldn't do it without them. Also check out **iGo (www.igo.com).** They also have an incredible variety of products and support for mobile computing around the world. Contact information for both companies is on page 180.

TeleAdapt's pocket-sized Mobile Connectivity Guide *(available from their web site) provides lists of every country's telephone connector, country code, international direct dialing code, and power plug specifications.*

Foreign Issues

TeleAdapt

toll free 877-835-3232
direct 408-965-1400
www.teleadapt.com
2151 O'Toole Avenue,
Suite H
San Jose, CA 95131

TeleAdapt also has
offices in Hong Kong,
Australia, and London.

Read through this information if you plan to connect your iBook in a foreign country just so you'll be aware of the sorts of issues you'll need to deal with. Then call TeleAdapt and ask them to fit you with the accessories you'll need to connect successfully. You may need a different arrangement of accessories depending on the country or countries you plan to visit! Also check with iGo; they also have a catalog and a web site with lots of great travel accessories.

Again, a reminder not to let this chapter scare you. All you need is the correct information and a few accessories and you're set to go.

Also check Chapter 7 for information about email accounts that you can check anywhere in the world from any Internet cafe, friend's house, office, or your laptop simply by getting on the Internet and using any browser. You can even arrange to check your America Online mail through a web page in case the computer you use doesn't have AOL software on it.

Power Adapter

The **power adapter** is that little box on your power cord between the wall plug and the computer connection. You'll notice on the back of the adapter are the specifications "AC 100–240V." That means you can use this power supply in any AC outlet in any country that uses from 100 volts to 240 volts in their electrical system, which covers every country in the world. So your power adapter/supply is one thing you don't have to worry about—Apple took care of it for you. Many PC laptop owners aren't so fortunate. (If you don't know the difference between AC and DC, please see the glossary.)

Hertz

Hertz (abbreviated as **Hz**) refers to the cycles per second of electrical current. In North America (including Canada and Mexico), the AC outlets operate at 60 Hertz, while many other countries use 50 Hertz. Your iBook can accommodate 50–60 Hertz, as indicated in the specifications on the back of the power supply (see above). So you don't need to worry about the difference in current cycles—Apple took care of it for you.

Surge Protector

You should use a **surge protector** in every country, including North America, to protect your iBook from the electrical surges that happen all the time. Both TeleAdapt and iGo sell portable ones that are great for home and travel, and you can use the same one in every country.

The **power plug** is the thing you plug into the wall. Very few countries use the same wall sockets that we use in North America, so you definitely must get a power plug adapter before you leave home. To make things more complicated, many countries have more than one power plug standard.

This "adapter" doesn't *convert* anything (such as voltage); it just adapts your power plug to fit into a strange socket. You stick your existing plug into the adapter, and the adapter plugs into the wall socket.

You must get a power plug adapter before you leave home. You can find power plug adapters for some countries at many travel stores. TeleAdapt has the correct adapters for every country in the world, plus they have packages that include the various adapters you'll need for an entire continent.

In North America, the standard **telephone connector** is called an RJ-11, and it's a "modular" connector. There are about forty other connectors around the world, so for connecting in many countries you must get a phone jack adapter. This adapter works like the power plug mentioned above—you plug the adapter into the wall, then plug the modem cable into the adapter.

You can get adapters in **duplex,** which means there are two sockets— one for the foreign telephone, and one for your RJ-11 modem cable. This is handy for times when you need access to the telephone, perhaps for manual dialing (like to connect with a calling card or because you need operator assistance), at the same time as you need modem access.

A **simplex** adapter has only one socket, and it's for your RJ-11 cable. If you find you need to manually dial the telephone while your modem is plugged in, you'll need a pocket phone (available from TeleAdapt) and one of those little "doublers" (shown to the right) that you can buy in any office supply store or sometimes in a large grocery store.

Even in the United States you'll run across phones that don't use the up-to-date modular RJ-11. That is, the phone lines may be "hard-wired" directly into the wall behind a little box (if you're as old as we are, you remember those well). This means there's no place at all for you to connect *any* sort of modem cable. But TeleAdapt even has solutions for this. As discussed in Chapter 9, you can get either a tool kit for connecting your modem cable directly to the wires, or a coupler and pocket phone to send the signals straight through a handset.

Power Plug

Telephone Connectors and Jacks

This is the standard RJ-11 connector we use in North America.

This is a common doubler. It lets you insert two RJ-11 cables into one socket.

Tax Impulsing

Many European countries use **tax impulsing** where a series of pulses measures the length of a phone call so it can be billed appropriately. These pulses can cause errors in the data transmissions and can even cause your modem to disconnect. If you plan to connect in a country that uses this system, you need a **line filter** (available from TeleAdapt and iGo) that will block out the tax impulse signals. The same filter works with all of the phone jack adapters.

TeleAdapt can tell you if the country you plan to visit uses tax impulsing. If you're already in that country, you can make a quick check for yourself: make a local call, and if you hear beeps at regular intervals, the phone most likely has tax impulsing.

Dial Tone

Your American modem probably won't recognize a foreign **dial tone** and so it won't dial. You'll need to tell the modem to **ignore the dial tone.** In the Modem control panel, check the box to "Ignore dial tone."

Reverse Polarity

You might run into phone lines with **reverse polarity,** as discussed in Chapters 8 and 9 (it can also happen in the States). Reverse polarity is where the four wires in the phone connection from the wall are in the reverse order from what the modem expects. It won't hurt your modem to plug into a socket with reverse polarity, but it probably won't work. TeleAdapt has a device that fixes this problem. We ran into a phone system with this situation and wished we had this device.

Digital Phone Lines

Very often the hotel switchboard uses a digital phone system, or the connections in a large corporate office are very likely to be digital. **Digital phone lines** cause the same problems in other countries as they do in North America. You need a *line tester* to check for the digital current, and a *digital converter* to plug your modem cable into. See Chapters 8 and 9 for more details.

Pulse Phone Lines

If you're old enough to know better, you probably remember phones that use a pulse instead of a tone. You had to turn the big, round dial for each number (which is why we call it "dialing" the phone, for those of you who have never seen one). Your modem much prefers the tone phones. **Pulse phone lines** cause the same problems in other countries as they do in North America. Be sure to choose the "Pulse" option in your Modem control panel.

It's very likely you'll need to use a calling card in a foreign country because in many places the closest "local" access number or ISP might still be a long-distance call. The basic pre-paid phone card that you buy in the local grocery store or from a local company is usually for calls made within the United States—it won't work when you leave the country. You must have an **international calling card,** available from Sprint, MCI, or AT&T, and some pre-paid phone cards.

To connect to the *States* from a foreign country (like to dial into your office email from Bulgaria), to connect to a long-distance number in the *same* foreign country, or to call from one foreign country to another, you need a **special access code** instead of the 800 number you are accustomed to using. When you order your international calling card, ask for a list of access codes—every vendor provides a list on a handy, calling-card sized card; in fact, you can even find these lists in the magazines on international planes. If you didn't get the access codes before you left home and you're already in a foreign country, look on the back of your calling card. There may be a number you can call collect to get the access codes you need.

Knowing you can get local access numbers for local Internet service providers all over the world (see page 136), you might think you never need to have your modem call long distance. Wrong. For instance, in Mexico the only "local" access number for the MindSpring service is in Mexico City; from Playa del Carmen in the Yucatan, that's still a long-distance call. How do you think we discovered this problem?

If you already have in your pocket a calling card from Sprint, MCI, or AT&T, check to see if it has an international PIN and authorization code printed on the front. This PIN (personal identification number) is only used when calling *from one foreign country to another.* That is, don't use that number if you are in a foreign country calling the States, nor to make a long distance call within that same country. Use it when you are calling from, say, Sweden to Spain.

Check the web sites for Sprint **(www.sprint.com),** MCI **(www.mci.com),** and AT&T **(www.att.com)** for information about their international calling cards and other services they might offer travelers.

See Chapters 8 and 9 for details about **how to use the calling card numbers** with your modem. You need to be aware of using **commas** to create pauses in the dialing string, and the possibility that you might have to use the telephone to manually dial and then switch the connection to your modem.

International Calling Cards

International Internet Accounts

Read Chapters 6 and 7 about alternative Internet service providers. We discuss getting an account with a company like EarthLink or Mind-Spring which provides local access numbers all over the country. EarthLink's reasonable rates are limited to the continental US, but MindSpring has a partnership with GRIC (a global internet roaming provider) that provides local numbers all over the world so you can log into an affiliated provider just about anywhere on earth and access your account. Check out their web site at **www.gric.com,** or call them at 408-955-1920.

Once you sign up for an international account with MindSpring, make sure to **get the list of local access numbers** *before* you leave the country! You can download it straight to your iBook. (If by chance you didn't get the numbers, you may have to connect to your home account with a long-distance number just long enough to go to the GRIC web site and find the local numbers for the area you are in.)

Web-Based Email

Read Chapters 6 and 7 about email accounts and the advantages of having web-based email that you can check anywhere in the world.

America Online around the world

If you use **America Online,** sign up for AOLNet before you leave home so you can check your email on any computer that is connected to the Internet and uses a browser (such as Netscape or Internet Explorer), even if the computer doesn't have the AOL software. To sign up with AOLNet, go to **www.aol.com/netmail.**

Check the Number

Since setting up the dialing process and actually making a connection through your iBook can be frustrating and time-consuming, do a quick check to verify that the modem number you want to call is the correct number. Call the other modem or fax number on the regular telephone and when you hear it connect (when you hear the modem or fax squeal), hang up. At least that will eliminate the possibility that the phone number is wrong so if things aren't working you won't spend hours trying to connect to a wrong number that isn't even a modem or fax line! It also verifies that all of your numbers are correct (like the calling card numbers) and that, if you could connect properly, the call would actually go through. Don't forget those commas that are so necessary when using a calling card or credit card; see pages 90–91 and 157–158.

Check for Surcharges

When calling from a foreign hotel, there is often an additional charge (a surcharge) for a long-distance call in addition to the long-distance call itself. To avoid a nasty surprise, call the front desk and ask.

It's possible to connect some Mac laptops (not the iBook) to the Internet through **cell phones** and surf, check email, send faxes, etc. But don't go thinkin' you can take your American analog (as opposed to digital) cell phone to foreign countries and connect. In fact, you can't even use your analog or digital cell phone in other countries to make *phone* calls.

In the United States, cell phones operate on a network that is some form of AMPS (Advanced Mobile Phone System), such as N-AMPS (narrowband), D-AMPS (digital), or the current standard E-AMPS (extended). The rest of the world uses GSM (Global System for Mobile Communications) or, in Japan, PDC (Personal Digital Cellular).

If you plan to connect via cell phone anywhere else in the world, go to the GSM web site **(www.gsmworld.com)** and find out how you can buy or rent a GSM phone and what you need to do to connect your PowerBook (can't connect your iBook yet) to the Internet or your company's intranet with it. It can get tricky because there are at least three differ-ent GSM frequencies (all different from the GSM that is starting to be used in the States), and if your phone is on one frequency but you end up in a country using a different frequency, you may have to transfer what's called your "identity module" from one phone to another.

Since if you plan to connect anywhere else in the world you need to call or contact TeleAdapt or iGo anyway, ask them about using a cell phone around the world, and tell them exactly what kind of Mac laptop you have. They can advise you on the best options.

If you're going to be in another country for several months or more and even MindSpring and GRIC can't get you a close-enough access number, sign up with a **local Internet service provider.** To find an ISP before you leave, go to **www.thelist.com.** The List provides contact information for almost 8,000 ISPs around the world.

On your iBook, use **Remote Access** and **DialAssist** to set up configurations for different places, as explained in detail on pages 157–158. You can enter the country codes, access codes, tell your modem to ignore the dial tone, etc., in one neat package. Then, when you want to connect from one place or another, simply use the Remote Access button in the control strip to choose the configuration you need. (If you switch to a different Internet service provider in other places, you'll need to change your TCP/IP information also.)

Cell Phone Connections Overseas

Use a Local ISP

Remote Access Configurations

To Sum it all Up

From our experience of connecting in odd parts of the world, this is what we recommend you do before you leave home and which peripheral devices we found we needed.

- Get a web-based email account, preferably one you can use to check all of your email accounts from.
- If you use AOL, get an AOLNet account.
- If you use an international provider, get their international list of phone numbers. If you have a Palm Organizer, see if the list is available as a downloadable file you can store in your Palm.
- If you plan to use a calling card, get an international one and make sure you have the access codes for the countries you plan to visit.
- Get a couple of phone connector doublers, available from your local office supply store, friendly telephone service person, or TeleAdapt or iGo.

From TeleAdapt or iGo:

- Get the power plug adapter and the telephone jack adapter you'll need for the country you're visiting. You may need to get more than one, depending on where you're going.
- Get a surge protector. Or get several since once it blows out, you have to replace it.
- Get a line tester to check for digital lines and reverse polarity.
- Find out if you need a line filter for tax impulsing in the country you plan to visit.
- Invest in a polarity reverse adapter (we wish we had done this earlier). It's really annoying to have reverse polarity be the easily-fixable thing that prevents your connection.
- If you think you may have to manually dial, get a pocket phone.
- We really like the retractable spool that holds 8.5 feet of ultra-thin modem cable. It's especially great on airplanes—your cord doesn't make a tangled mess.
- If you think you might need to connect from pay phones, old pulse phones, or analog hard-wired wall jacks, get the acoustic coupler, a handset that straps to the phone handset and has a cable that connects to your modem. See Chapters 8 and 9.
- Buy the *Mobile Connectivity Guide* from TeleAdapt, study it before you go, and take it with you.
- If it's important that your connections work, get TeleAdapt's tech support package—24/7 around the world.

TeleAdapt

toll free 877-835-3232
direct 408-965-1400
www.teleadapt.com
2151 O'Toole Avenue,
Suite H
San Jose, CA 95131

TeleAdapt also has offices in Hong Kong, Australia, and London.

iGo

toll free 888-350-4090
direct 775-746-6140
www.igo.com
2301 Robb Drive
Reno, NV 89523

Part IV
Extras

This section provides a bunch of extra tips, discusses some of the many accessories you can get to add to your iBook to make it even more useful to you, and contains a glossary of all the terms we used in this book that may be new to you. And of course, the index.

Fantasy
Working by the pool

Reality
iBlanket accessory
necessary for working by the pool

Extra iBook Tips

Now that you know how to connect all over your house and all over the world, here are a few extra tips, whether you are traveling from Arkansas to Baghdad, from your home office to the living room, or sitting quietly in your tree fort.

Here's Robin's favorite tip: **Turn off that talking lady.** You know, the one who reads the alerts out loud to you.

To turn off the talking lady (or man), use the Speech control panel

1. Open the Speech control panel.
2. In the little Options menu, choose "Talking Alerts."
3. Uncheck "Speak the phrase" and "Speak the alert text."

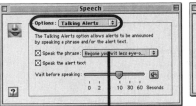 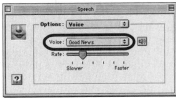

In this menu you'll find options to edit existing phrases and create your own.

This is really a fun control panel to play with: On someone else's computer, make a new phrase in the "Talking Alerts" section, something like, "Begone you witless eye-offending parasitic goober," then check the box to "Speak the phrase," and set the timing to 0 (zero). In the "Voice" section, choose a nasty voice. Everytime the computer would normally beep at that person using the computer, this phrase will be read out loud instead. Very few people know how to turn it off. Url told you this, not us.

Power Conservation Tips

If you need to make the most of your battery power, here are ten tips that will help maximize your battery's life.

1. Reduce the screen's brightness (use the F1 key).

2. If there's a CD in the CD drive, remove it.

3. In the Energy Saver control panel, click "Advanced Settings."
   From the menu labeled "Settings for," choose "Battery."
   Check the box to "Allow processor cycling."

4. Set the iBook to sleep after a short period of inactivity:

   In the Energy Saver control panel, click the "Sleep Setup" button.
   From the menu labeled "Settings for," choose "Battery."
   Move the "Energy Use" slider all the way to the left toward "Better Conservation."

5. Turn off AppleTalk when you're not using it (you need it when sharing files or printing to a PostScript printer):

   a. From the Apple menu, slide down to "Control Panels" and choose "AppleTalk."

   b. In the AppleTalk control panel, click the "Options..." button in the bottom-right corner.

      If the "Options..." button is not visible, go to the Edit menu and choose "User Mode...." Select "Advanced," then click OK. Now the "Options..." button is visible and you can click it to open the "AppleTalk Options" dialog box.

   c. Check "Inactive" to turn AppleTalk off. Click OK.

6. Disconnect any external devices that you're not using, such as Zip drives or printers.

7. Quit any applications you're not using.

8. If you have an AirPort Card, turn its power off when it's not in use. Use the AirPort Card control panel to do so.

9. Plug in your computer whenever possible so your battery stays charged and ready to use.

10. Save the files you're working on to a RAM disk, which is a portion of your computer's memory that you allocate for use as a high-speed storage disk. Besides being energy efficient, it's blazingly fast.

To create a RAM disk

a. Open the Memory control panel.

b. Click the "RAM Disk" option to "On."

c. **Very important:** Check the box for "Save on Shut Down." If you don't check this box, any work you've saved to the RAM disk will be erased when you shut down, unless you manually saved the contents of the RAM disk back to your hard disk or to an external drive.

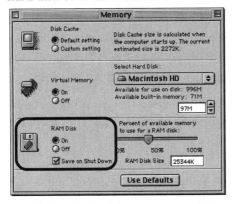

d. Restart. Although there is no clue warning you in the control panel, the RAM disk won't actually appear on your Desktop until you restart.

e. After restart, a disk icon labeled RAM disk (shown below) will appear on your Desktop for you to use just like any other disk. Save files to this RAM disk, delete files, or drag files to and from the RAM disk.

This is the RAM disk icon you'll see. Use it like any other disk, keeping in mind the contents are actually in RAM, so back up your documents regularly to your real hard disk.

f. To delete a RAM disk, first copy everything from it onto your hard disk. Then go back to the Memory control panel and check the "Off" button. If file sharing is turned on, you can't turn off the RAM disk, so if necessary, turn off file sharing.

System Software Troubleshooting

Pack your iBook's System Software CD with your jammies when you travel. Occasionally system software corruptions will make a computer act so goofy that your only option is to force the computer to restart with the startup software on the System Software CD. And if you've ever needed to reinstall system software while you were away from home, you'll appreciate how great it is to have the right CD with you.

To restart from the system CD

1. Insert the disk into the CD drive.

2. Choose "Restart" from the Special menu, and hold down the letter C key. This forces the iBook to start up from the CD.

   If you are so stuck you can't choose anything from a menu, hold down the Control and Command keys and hit the Power button to restart. Immediately press and hold the C key.

3. Once the iBook has started and is running normally, you can do your regular troubleshooting stuff to see if you can find out what's wrong with your system.

Rebuild the Desktop

Even if you can't figure out the problem, **rebuild the Desktop.** Rebuilding the Desktop can solve an amazing multitude of problems:

1. Hold down the Shift, Option, and Command keys as you restart. (The Shift key actually turns off the system extensions and prevents them from loading, which gives you a little cleaner rebuild).

2. Hold these three keys down until a dialog box appears on your screen asking if you're sure you want to rebuild the Desktop. Click "Yes." A progress bar will indicate when the computer has finished.

3. Finally, restart the iBook again without holding down any keys.

Unreliable Modem Connections

If you're having trouble maintaining modem connections, it may be caused by low-quality, noisy phone lines. When phone line quality is marginal, slower connections are more reliable. Try selecting a slower modem connection speed:

1. Open the Modem control panel.

2. From the Modem menu in the control panel, choose "Apple Internal 56K Modem (v.34)" instead of the default choice of "Apple 56K Modem (v.90)."

Some airlines provide a limited number of seats with 12v DC power supplies so passengers can plug in their laptops and work without draining their batteries. If you register with TeleAdapt's AirPower Database (go to **teleadapt.com**), they'll keep you posted on all airline seats that offer powered seats. To plug in to that power source, you'll need an airline adapter like the kind you can find at **teleadapt.com** or **iGo.com.** You can get a straight airline adapter, or you can get a piece that connects onto the end of an auto adapter (the kind you plug into the car cigarette lighter) so you can use the same tool for both the car ride to the airport and the plane ride.

Airline Travel

Look for **Laptop Lanes** in major airports. They've installed 40-square-foot Smart Office workstations with 7-foot-high walls and lockable doors. Each Smart Office has a power source, modem, desktop PC (Windows), and a T1 connection (that's a very fast connection) to the Internet. Each office even has a printer, fax machine, and conference-call capable phone. Not bad for 38¢ a minute ($22.80 an hour). If you have questions while working in the Smart Office, you can ask the cyber-concierge. Check their web site **(www.laptoplane.com)** for locations and details.

Laptop Lanes and Smart Offices

When you're trying to catch a flight, the security gate always makes you boot up your laptop to make sure it's not a bomb. It can be very frustrating to wait for your computer to startup since you have to wait until it gets all the way to the Desktop before you can shut it down. But waking up from **Sleep** is much faster than a whole startup. So before you get to the airport, start up your iBook and put it into Sleep mode. When a guard at the security station asks you to boot the computer, it will take just a few seconds for the screen to light up. As soon as security gives you clearance, shut the cover of the iBook to put it back to sleep and continue on your way.

Airport Security

When going through the security gates, always pass your computer around the side to the guard. It's actually not the x-rays that can cause grief to your computer data—it's the magnets that are usually in the motor that drives the belt that goes through the x-ray machine. Try to avoid putting your iBook on the belt, but if you must, take it off as quickly as possible. Same goes for the belt that brings your luggage out to you—it can hurt your computer. Not that you'd want to send your beautiful new laptop through the luggage system anyway.

Watch the rollers

Theft and security Last year over 850 laptops were stolen EACH DAY, many from airports. This means several things to you:

◆ Password-protect your important or personal data on your iBook so in case it's stolen, it won't be easy for someone to get into your files. Unfortunately, the Password Security control panel specifically for PowerBooks is no longer available (well, it's available but it won't work on the iBook), so you'll have to buy some third-party software if you want good protection. In the upcoming Mac OS update, you'll have built-in voice imprint password protection.

◆ If you take your iBook out of town a lot, invest in some anti-theft hardware. Check any computer catalog, as well as **teleadapt.com** and **iGo.com.**

◆ Since so many laptops are stolen, it's not a bad idea to take your proof of purchase with your serial number as you travel. That way if your iBook needs servicing, you won't be suspected of having stolen the machine. Or if your iBook is stolen, you can prove the machine is yours or at least put the serial number in the police report.

Pardon my French What if you're in Germany, France, Portugal, Italy, or Spain and you suddenly remember you forgot to learn German, French, Portuguese, Italian, or Spanish before you left home. Log on to **http://babelfish. altavista.com** where you can enter any text into a dialog box, choose a language, and get a free translation of the text. Since the translation is machine-produced, you shouldn't rely completely on it, but it can be a big help. Instead of entering a phrase, you can also type a web address into the dialog box and choose which languages you want that web page to be translated from and into.

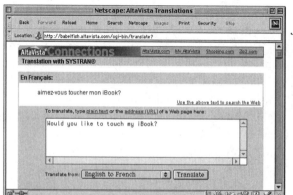

This is really fun. It could be a great icebreaker with strangers in a foreign country.

If you don't want to go online for translations, buy translation software, such as Word Translator from Translation Experts Limited **(www.tranexp.com).** Their CD includes English, French, Spanish, German, Swedish, Danish, Norwegian, Finnish, Russian, Polish, and Portuguese. As long as you're carrying your iBook around the world anyway, why not carry a dozen or so language dictionaries with you?

A backpack will suffice for carrying your iBook around, but a good computer carrying case specifically designed for laptops is even better, especially if you're carrying extra gadgets and adapters. John uses a Timberland bag that has extra padding for the laptop, plenty of extra storage space, lots of pockets for adapters, and a comfortable shoulder strap. If you prefer a travel case with wheels, they're available also.

Invest in a Travel Bag

An auto power adapter accessory makes it possible to use your iBook in the car without depleting battery power. Use the auto adapter to charge the iBook's battery. Buy a street map CD and use the iBook to find your way around. Let your kids play Bugdom in the back seat. Or play Bugdom in the backseat yourself while your roomie drives.

Car Travel

You can get an adapter from **iGo.com** that plugs into your car cigarette lighter and lets you plug *three* devices into the one source (it's called a Socket Multiplier). So you can keep your cell phone and your laptop working at the same time. Hey, you could plug in your cell phone, plug in your laptop, connect your laptop to the cell phone, and carry on your Internet love affairs while on your road trip! And if you're going to do that, you might as well get the LapTraveler from iGo, a portable "desk" for the passenger seat.

This is an auto adapter that lets your computer (or many other devices) plug into the cigarette lighter in the car. Make sure you get a model that fits your iBook.

iBook Screen Resolution

You'll find that if you select a **screen resolution** of 640 x 480, it won't look as sharp as the default resolution of 800 x 600. This is due to the limitations of the digital LCD screen on the iBook. The only reason Apple added the option to change the resolution is because some games will only play at 640 x 480. So if you do change the resolution and it looks kind of blurry, don't think you have a bad screen—that's just what happens.

Staying Informed

Wouldn't it be nice if someone checked around every day and let you know what software upgrades are available and where to get them? That's exactly what you get when you visit some of the Macintosh-focused sites that are on the World Wide Web. Keep up with the latest news, software updates, cool freeware, and great shareware. Get timely information about hardware and software problems and solutions. There are dozens of sites to choose from, and John checks at least a half dozen every day. Some of our favorite sites for staying informed are:

MacInTouch	www.macintouch.com
The iBook Zone	www.ibookzone.com
MacAddict	www.macaddict.com
AppleInsider	www.appleinsider.com
Macintosh News Network	www.macnn.com
Macworld Online	macworld.zdnet.com
MacWeek	www.macweek.com
MacCentral Online	www.maccentral.com
MacHome Interactive	www.machome.com
Apple	www.apple.com

Emergency Resurrection

If you drop your iBook, it gets crushed in an earthquake, sinks to the bottom of the muddy Nile, gets burnt in a fire, or run over by a truck, don't despair. Call **Drive Savers.** They can't make your machine workable again if it's been run over by a truck, but they can get the data off of the drive. They are truly amazing and also very nice people.

Call them in Novato, California, at 800.440.1904, or go to their web site at **www.drivesavers.com.**

Accessories 13

The iBook is remarkable all by itself, but you can increase its productivity and your enjoyment by adding peripherals and accessories to it.

For instance, how about a mouse? Even if you love the trackpad on your iBook, you might find times when you really want a mouse. You can buy one and attach it to your iBook.

If you're leaving town, also check Chapter 8 for accessories that are not only good to have, but some that are critical if you plan to connect away from your home base.

In this chapter, we mention a product and then, in bold, you see a list of manufacturers who make the product. A contact list for the manufacturers is on page 193.

Converter Cables and Adapters for Connecting Non-USB Devices

Most accessories you get for the iBook will have USB connectors. USB (Universal Serial Bus) is the type of connector the iBook uses to connect other devices. But you may want to connect to existing peripherals that don't have a USB connector.

You can connect the iBook to non-USB devices if you have the right adapters. Several companies make the adapters that enable you to connect peripherals that use serial ports, parallel ports, or SCSI ports. This includes certain digital cameras, scanners, graphic tablets, etc. These adapters are referred to as USB-to-serial, USB-to-parallel, USB-to-Ethernet, and USB-to-SCSI adapters.

Ariston Technologies, Belkin, CompuCable, Entrega, Griffin Technologies, Interex, Keyspan, Microtech International

Resources

The resources listed here are not intended to be a complete list, but just a sampling of the products and manufacturers that can enhance your iBook experience. Some of these manufacturers sell products on their own web sites, but many of them provide links to online catalogs and warehouses.

Hardware and software online catalogs

MacWarehouse	800.255.6277	www.warehouse.com
MacConnection	800.800.2222	www.macconnection.com
MacMall	800.328.2790	www.macmall.com
Computer Discount Warehouse	800.844.4239	www.cdw.com
Small Dog Electronics	802.496.7171	www.smalldog.com

Products for mobile computing

These companies have products specifically for mobile computing.

TeleAdapt	877.835.3232	www.teleadapt.com
iGo	888.350.4090	www.igo.com

Information and product resource for USB and peripherals

These are great online sources for USB and peripherals.

Apple	www.apple.com
MacInTouch	www.macintouch.com/imacusb.html

Note on USB Compatibility

Don't believe it when the salesperson swears that anything called "USB" will work on the Mac—not all devices are compatible. We know this. Make sure the product you buy really is truly compatible with the Mac platform.

3Com	408.326.5000	www.palm.com
Agfa	888.281.2302	www.agfahome.com
APS Tech	800.395.5871	www.apstech.com
Ariston Technologies	800.326.5294	www.ariston.com
AVerMedia	800.863.2332	www.aver.com
Avid Technologies	800.949.2843	www.avidtech.com
Belkin Components	800.233.5546	www.belkin.com
CompuCable	800.344.6921	www.compucable.com
CH products	760.598.2518	www.chproducts.com
Entrega Technologies	949.859.8866	www.entrega.com
Epson	800.463.7766	www.epson.com
Griffin Technologies	800.986.6578	www.griftech.com
Hewlett-Packard	800.522.8500	www.hp.com
iMaccessories	888.622.8355	www.imaccessories.com
Imation	888.466.3456	www.imation.com
Infowave Software Inc.	800.663.6222	www.infowave.com
Interex	877.468.3739	www.interexinc.com
Kensington	800.280.8318	www.kensington.com
Keyspan	510.222.0131	www.keyspan.com
Kodak	800.235.6325	www.kodak.com
LaCie	800.999.0670	www.lacie.com
Logitech	800.231.7717	www.logitech.com
Macally	800.644.1132	www.macally.com
Microtech Intl.	800.626.4276	www.microtechint.com
Microtek	800.654.4160	www.microtekusa.com
Newer Technology	316.943.0222	www.newertech.com
Umax Technologies	800.562.0311	www.umax.com
Wacom	800.922.6613	www.wacom.com
Winstation	800.243.3475	www.winstation.com

*OEMs
(Original Equipment
Manufacturers)*

USB Hubs

A USB hub is a device that adds additional USB ports to your iBook for connecting extra peripherals, such as scanners, printers, joysicks, etc. Hubs come in a variety of sizes, determined by the number of USB ports on the hub.

Ariston, Belkin, CompuCable, Entregra, iMaccessories, Interex, Keyspan, Newer Technology

Palm Computing Connected Organizers

For those times when the iBook is just too cumbersome, take along one of these palm-sized Personal Digital Assistants (PDA). You'll stay organized with the same Palm Organizer software that's on your iBook and you can synchronize, backup, and exchange files between the Palm Organizer and the iBook. The Palm Organizer won't do everything the iBook can do, but you'll be able to customize it by choosing from thousands of available shareware and freeware personal productivity applications. From **3Com.**

USB Mice

The trackpad is convenient for traveling light or working in a tight space. But most of us are more comfortable using a mouse. If you want to use a mouse, you'll need to get a USB mouse to fit into the USB connector on side of the iBook. They're available from many computer stores, online warehouses, and manufacturers.

Ariston, Belkin, CompuCable, iMaccessories, Interex, Kensington, Logitech, MacAlly

USB Game Pads and Joysticks

If you're seriously into computer games, you'll definitely want one of these devices to maximize your scoring.

Ariston, CHProducts, iMaccessories, Kensington, Logitech, Macally

USB Scanners and Printers

There are many USB scanners and printers to choose from, including a couple of combination scanner/printer/copier machines.

Agfa, CompuCable, Epson, Hewlett-Packard, Microtek, Umax Technologies

Video Capture

AVerMedia's USBpresenter is an iBook-to-TV converter that brings video output to the iBook so you can use it for presentations.

iView, from Ariston, is a USB video capture device for digitizing video from TV or home video cameras.

Avid Cinema software from Avid Technologies includes a USB video capture device.

If you want a microphone to record into or if the built-in speaker just isn't quite powerful enough, you can add your own external speakers or microphone.

Ariston Technologies, Griffin Technologies, CompuCable

Also, IBM Corporation is preparing a version of its ViaVoice headset that will connect to a USB port. ViaVoice is IBM's speech recognition technology.

External Microphone and Speakers

Although the iBook automatically charges its battery when using the AC power adapter, you may want to charge more than one battery at a time, or you may want an extra battery or two to take on trips, in which case you'll need a battery charger. Since the iBook uses a new kind of battery, be sure you get the right kind, a Lithium-Ion battery.

Apple, VST Technologies

Batteries and Battery Chargers

You can never have too much hard drive space. USB external hard drives can give you huge amounts of much needed extra storage. Some even come in iBook colors.

APS, LaCie, VST Technologies

USB Hard Drives

Yes, some people still use floppies. As a matter of fact, they're essential for some people. The 1.4 MB USB floppy drives and 120 MB USB SuperDisk floppy drives are available if you have a need for them.

Ariston, iMaccessories, Imation, Microtech, Newer Technology, VST Technologies

USB Floppy Drives

USB Zip Drives come in storage capacities of 100 MB and 250 MB. Zip disks are one of the most popular solutions for storing and transporting large files.

Iomega, Microtech International, Winstation

USB Zip Drives

Surge protectors prevent power surges in the electric lines from harming your computer. For our laptops, we like the small, portable type. There are a variety of types, so check around.

TeleAdapt, iGo, catalogs

Portable Surge Protector

USB Cameras

Several companies make the cute little cameras that sit on top of your screen and can be used to capture a video clip or still images. These cameras are often used as web cams, either for security monitoring, video conferencing, or just for fun.

Ariston, Logitech

If you want a USB digital camera that looks, feels, and acts more like a traditional camera, Kodak has just what you're looking for. However, if you have a USB card reader, you're not limited to using a USB camera. A USB card reader is a device that attaches to the iBook's USB port and can read the small memory cards used by digital cameras (Compact Flash cards or SmartMedia cards).

Compact Flash and SmartMedia Card Readers

Compact Flash cards and SmartMedia cards are postage-sized cards that are usually used with digital cameras (as noted above), but can also be used as storage media if you have a USB Compact Flash reader or a USB SmartMedia card reader.

Iomega, Microtech, Newer Technology

Auto and Plane Power Adapters

Special power adapters for automobile and airplanes enable you to use your iBook while you're traveling without worrying about the battery power running out. The auto adapter plugs into the car cigarette lighter, and the plane adapter plugs into special sockets on the back of some seats on some airplanes (see the tip on page 187 about airline travel).

TeleAdapt, iGo, catalogs, office supply stores

Retractable Modem Cable

Retractable modem cables are one of the accessories that you shouldn't live without, even if you never leave home with your iBook. It's a wonderful alternative to carrying around a 10-foot phone card.

TeleAdapt, iGo, catalogs, office supply stores

Glossary 14

Included in this glossary are the terms we have used in this book that may be unfamiliar to you. Any noun you see in italic is also defined elsewhere in the glossary. If you need more information on anything, try one of these solutions:

- If you don't find the word listed, check the index to see if it's explained within another definition or somewhere else in the book.

- If you are brand-new to computers, get *The Little iMac Book*. This is a tutorial-oriented book specifically for brand-new computer users that will even teach you how to use the AppleWorks software you have on your iBook. After you read that book, everything will make more sense.

- If you have been using a Mac for a little while but are still a bit confused about what is going on in your machine and how to control it, and if you want all the tips and tricks about everything in your Mac, read *The Little Mac Book*.

- There is a simple-to-understand glossary about Internet stuff written by Robin at Url's Internet Cafe. Go to **www.UrlsInternetCafe.com/glossary.**

- For an incredibly complete dictionary of every term you might ever hear in the computer and Internet world, go to **www.whatis.com.** This site is a great resource. If you look up a term and it's not in their list, tell them and they'll add that definition.

AC AC stands for alternating current, which is the kind of electric power we have in our houses. Almost all computers, however, use DC, or direct current. That little box in the middle of the power cord on your iBook adapts the AC power into the appropriate DC power for the computer. Desktop computers have a power supply inside the box that does the same thing.

adapters The term **adapter** has several meanings in the computer world. The one we use in this book refers to a small device that adapts one sort of plug to fit into a socket. For instance, in a foreign country, your iBook power plug won't fit into the wall socket. So you need to put an adapter on your power plug, and stick the adapter into the foreign wall socket. An adapter doesn't change anything—it just makes something fit.

You might also hear the term adapter refer to a *card* that you insert into certain computers to add extra features or to control extra devices.

alias An **alias,** on a Mac, is an icon you create that, when you double-click it, goes and gets another file (such as a document, folder, application, or control panel). The advantage of an alias is that you can keep all of your files organized into their folders (many applications won't work if you take them out of their folders), yet keep their aliases handy right on the Desktop. You can make multiple aliases and store them in separate places; for instance, perhaps you want a budget report stored in the office folder, in the monthly folder, and in the tax folder. Instead of storing multiple copies of the file, which then might not all get updated correctly, store aliases. Each alias will open the original file.

Acrobat Catalog

You can always tell if an icon is an alias because its name is in italic.

analog According to Guy Kawasaki, one of the original Apple evangelists, **analog** is anything you can read in direct sunlight. (Don't get excited about the hype you hear of using your iBook by the pool—just like your digital watch in direct sun, you won't be able to see anything on the computer screen.)

Analog refers to things in the world that are infinite and flowing, like time and sound and water and wind. You can keep dividing analog items into smaller and smaller pieces forever.

The opposite of analog is *digital.* Digital refers to things you can count in finite chunks, like your fingers (digits). Think of water (analog) as compared to ice cubes (digital). Think of a regular, old-fashioned watch with a second hand (analog) as compared to a digital watch that flips from one second to the next with nothing between. The computer is digital; your mind is analog.

AOL : **AOL** is an abbreviation for **America Online,** the world's largest online service. AOL provides email, chat rooms, downloadable software, clubs, and much more. You could probably decorate your Christmas tree with all the free disks you've gotten in the mail.

AppleScript : **AppleScript** is a scripting language, which is sort of like a programming language, that makes small events happen. Many applications call on AppleScripts to make things happen in their software, and you can even write your own scripts to automate events on your iBook. For instance, you can write a script that shows up in the *contextual menu* that will send a certain file into a certain folder.

For all the gory details, go to the *Finder* (also called the *Desktop*), and from the Help menu choose "Mac OS Help." Type in the world "applescript" and hit Return. You'll find lots of information. For even more info, go to the web site **www.apple.com/applescript.**

archive : An **archive** is a file or collection of files that has been saved and set aside for posterity, or at least until you need them again. You keep archives in a safe place, not on your hard disk (if it's on your hard disk, it's not really an archive). Typically, the word implies that the files have also been *compressed* all together into one neat package so you can fit more onto the storage media (disk).

ASCII : ASCII (pronounced "ass kee") stands for American Standard Code for Information Interchange. ASCII is the one thing that all the various sorts of computers can read—it's the bottom level of character code. This means if you save a file in ASCII format (which is the same as "text" or "text only"), you can send it to anyone on any computer and they can read it. It's pretty ugly, though. There's no formatting whatsover, not even bold or italic. But this lack of formatting is what makes designers prefer getting ASCII files from clients—the designers don't have to strip out all of the client's misguided attempts at formatting.

autodial : **Autodial** is when the modem itself dials the number to connect. The opposite of autodialing is *manual dialing,* where you use your fingers to dial the actual telephone and connect to the *server* and then transfer the call to the *modem.*

browser

Netscape Communicator

Internet Explorer

These are the icons for the browsers that are already installed on your iBook.

A **browser** is a specific software application that displays *web pages* on your iBook (or on any computer). Think of it like any other application: to write a letter, you use the application called a word processor; to keep a mailing list of contacts, you use a database application; to surf the web, you use a browser application.

You have two browsers on your iBook: Netscape Communicator (preferred by many) and Microsoft Internet Explorer (if you are willing to support Bill Gates and Microsoft; personally, I don't think he needs me). Use either one you choose. If you use America Online to get to the Internet, it will use its own browser; if you don't like that one, log on to AOL, then double-click your preferred browser.

To use a browser, it's best to first connect to the Internet, then open the browser. In the "Location" or "Go To" box at the very top of the browser window (not the box that says something like "search"), type in the web location of where you want to go, hit the Return key, and the browser will display that web page on your screen.

On your iBook, if you click the "Browse the Internet" icon you might see on your Desktop, it will connect to the Internet and open the browser for you **if** you have already set up your service with an *Internet service provider.*

bus

A **bus** is a collection of hardware, software, and wires that creates a way for all the different parts of your comptuer to communicate with each other. If there was no bus, you'd have wires coming and going everywhere. It would be like having a different wiring system for every lightbulb in your house.

The bus system on Macintoshes has been changing over the years, getting faster and faster. Your iBook has what's called a PCI bus.

card

A **card,** in computer jargon, is a small plastic piece that fits inside a slot in your computer. The purpose of a card is to provide more functions for your computer. Cards come in various sizes and do various things. They might be nine inches long and four inches wide, or they might be one inch square. See *PC card* for more details.

compression

To send files through the internet, we **compress** them, which makes them smaller in file size. If they are smaller in file size, they will go through the phone lines faster.

There are different kinds of compression "schemes." Some are called "lossless," in which no data is destroyed in the compression. Other schemes are "lossy," which means some data is lost and can never be

Scarlett'sFont.sit

Scarlett'sFont.hqx

The three-letter extensions at the end of these file names tell you these files are compressed.

retrieved, but it's data you usually won't notice, like the color might shift a bit in a graphic image.

All graphics on the web are compressed (or should be) so they download to your computer faster. Most of the files you attach to email should be compressed before you send them (see below). When you download software from the Internet, it is always compressed.

When you download a compressed file or get a compressed attachment, it must be uncompressed before you can use it or install it. Most of your software is set up to automatically uncompress files, but if it isn't, you can use the software on your iBook called StuffIt Expander. If the file has an *extension* of .sit or .hqx at the end of its name, you should be able to double-click on it, it will open StuffIt Expander, unstuff itself, and Expander will quit. Then you have to look carefully—you will find that the .sit or .hqx file is still on your Desktop (or wherever it was), which might make you think nothing happened. But look carefully, or use Sherlock Find File to search—there will be another file with a similar name without the .sit or .hqx extension! It might be a folder or it might be a file with a special icon. That is the uncompressed file. Once you find the uncompressed file, you can toss the .sit or .hqx in the trash. Also see the definition for *.sea*, which is another compression scheme.

Scarlett'sFont

After you uncompress the file, you'll find the regular icon. Once you have the unstuffed file, you can toss the stuffed ones away.

If by chance you download a file with an extension of .zip, that is an indication that the file is a PC file and was compressed on a PC. Stuffit Expander can usually unzip a zipped file, but if it's a PC file you still might not be able to open it once you unzip it, depending on what it is.

To compress files yourself for attaching or sending, you need to buy an application like StuffIt Deluxe or Compact Pro. Because StuffIt Deluxe is the most popular compression utility, we often say that compressed files are "stuffed."

contextual menu

On your iBook (or on any Mac running OS 8 or later), you can hold down the Control key (not the Command key!) and press on any file on the Desktop, like a folder or a document or a window, and a special little menu called a **contextual menu** will show up. Depending on what you click on, the contextual menu will have different options. One of our favorites is the "Move To Trash" option.

This is a contextual menu.

If you don't know about contextual menus, it's a clue that you really should read *The Little Mac Book.* Here's another clue: do you know how to open spring-loaded folders or use the click-and-a-half? If not, please read that book!

control panel

This is the Mouse control panel icon and the actual panel.

If you don't know what a **control panel** is, you need to read *The Little Mac Book*. You'll learn all about control panels and everything else.

A control panel is a small utility that adds extra features to your Mac. It's similar to an *extension* except that you have some control over its features. Under the Apple menu is a choice called "Control Panels." Take a look at that list. Each of those items does something special, and you can open each one and see which of its features you can control. For instance, if you choose "Apple Menu Options," you can determine whether the Apple menu displays "hierarchical menus" or not (hierarchical menus, or h-menus, are those that pop out to the side, indicated in the main menu by the tiny triangles pointing to the side).

cpu

The **cpu** (central processing unit) is actually the tiny chip inside the computer that runs everything. It's also called the processor. The cpu on the iBook is housed under the keyboard.

Because the cpu is always inside the main box that holds all the computer stuff, on a desktop computer we often call the box itself the cpu. For instance, your desktop computer system might consist of the "cpu," the monitor, the keyboard, and the mouse, where "cpu" refers to the boxy part with the ports on the back and the drive slots in the front.

data

Also see data port.

The term "tera" as in "terabyte" comes from the Greek word for monster.)

Data, in the sense we are using it in this book, means the information that is in or sent through the computer. A file going through the modem lines or a file sent to the printer to print is data. Data is stored in tiny electronic units called bits. Each bit is either a 1 (one) or a 0 (zero). Eight bits make one byte. 1,024 bytes make one kilobyte. 1,024 kilobytes make one gigabyte. 1,024 gigabytes make one terabyte.

Data is *digital*, as opposed to voice, which is *analog*. That's why when you connect your computer in some places (like on an airplane) and want to send an email, you are asked if it is data, fax, or voice you want to send. An email and its attachment are data.

A fax is sent through the lines as a complete image, so it goes through in a slightly different way from email or voice.

data port

A **data port** is a very important thing. If you have been in a fancy hotel, you might have noticed a telephone plug labeled "data port." This is because in fancy hotels, the *PBX* switchboard is usually *digital*, and if you plug your modem into their digital phone and try to connect, you will blow up your modem! Your modem's job is to translate digital data into *analog* to send it over phone lines, so the hotel provides an analog data port for your modem connection. Use it. Don't ever plug into a hotel telephone or a phone in a large office without first checking to see if it's digital or not. See Chapters 8 and 9 for more details

DC   **DC** stands for direct current. The electrical system in our houses and offices use AC, alternating current, but our computers use DC. So every desktop computer has a built-in power supply that converts the AC to DC. Laptops like your iBook, have an AC to DC adapter, or power supply, on the cord that goes between the wall socket and the laptop.

The power from the car cigarette lighter and the power sources in airplane seats are DC, but it's a different voltage than the computer uses so you still need a power cable with an adapter on it.

Desktop   In this book, **Desktop** with a capital D refers to the computer screen you see when you first start up the iBook—you see the trash can, the icon for your hard disk, and the word "Special" in the menu. The Desktop is like home base. This is where you keep all of your folders and applications, and this is where you go to trash files and shut down.

The Desktop is run by the software called the *Finder*, so you will often hear the terms Desktop and Finder interchanged. If someone or some directions tell you to go to the Finder, that is the same as telling you to go to the Desktop.

digital   **Digital** refers to finite, countable things, like fingers (digits). The computer works with digital information. Actually, the computer only works with two digital pieces: an off signal and an on signal. Each signal is called one bit. It takes eight bits (one byte) to make a typical character in a word processor. It's amazing what the computer can do with these bits of information. Every beautiful photo you see on the screen is composed of collections of these bits. The bigger the photo and the more colors in it, the more digital bits of information it takes to create it, which is why a photograph is a much bigger file size than a word processing document or an email.

See the definition for *analog*, which is the opposite of digital.

download   To **download** means to transfer a copy of a file *from* a (usually bigger) computer or system *to* your computer. For instance, you can download thousands of pieces of software through the Internet—the files are on another computer and you download them to yours.

drive   The **drive** is the mechanism that holds and spins a disk so you can get information from and copy information to the disk. You have a built-in hard drive in your iBook that runs your hard disk. Many Macs have built-in floppy drives or Zip drives.

Your iBook has a CD-ROM drive, but it doesn't have any extra *drive bays*. You can buy drives as *peripherals* that you attach to your iBook. For instance, you can buy a Zip drive or a floppy drive, and then you can use Zip disks and floppy disks.

drive bay   A **drive bay** is the slot in many portable computers where you can insert a variety of different drives. For instance, on the PowerBook G3, you can insert a Zip drive into the drive bay, a CD-ROM drive, or an extra hard drive. Only one drive at a time can fit in the bay, but you can swap them without turning off the computer. The iBook does not have a drive bay so the only way to use another drive is to attach it through your USB port.

driver   The **driver** is the piece of software that tells the computer how to communicate with an attached device. For instance, your printer needs a driver so when you choose to print, the iBook knows how to send the page to the printer properly.

Ethernet   **Ethernet** is a connection for two or more computers that allows information (data) to be sent from one place to another very quickly. An

Ethernet connector looks like the regular phone connector on the end of your telephone cord, except it's bigger (as shown to the left). The Ethernet port (socket) looks like a regular phone jack, except it's bigger.

You might connect an Ethernet cable between two or more computers, into a cable modem, into an AirPort wireless connection, or between other devices to transfer information back and forth quickly.

extension   There are two main definitions for extension. On the Macintosh, certain tiny files that the computer loads when it starts up are called **extensions.** They help the system run things, and they help certain applications accomplish certain features of their software. When your iBook first starts up and you see the tiny icons appear and disappear across the screen, those are extensions. Some extensions conflict with other extensions and can cause problems, which is why you have a *control panel* called Extensions Manager. The Extensions Manager lets you turn on or off any extensions or other control panels.

The other meaning of **extension** refers to the period (the dot) and the two to four letters you might see at the end of some file names, such as

scarlettt.sit

glossary.wd

ethernetcable.tif

These extensions help to identify the files.

.tif, .jpg, .html, .sit, .ai, or .hqx. The extension gives you a clue as to what sort of file it is. This feature is a holdover from PC machines because files on the PC must have the proper extension or dumb ol' Windows doesn't know what to do with them.

On the Mac, we sometimes use extensions not because we have to, but because it can help to identify our files. For instance, in a folder containing a chapter for a book, Robin always identifies word processing files with .wd, PageMaker files with .pm, and screen shots with .tif so in a folder she knows what they are even if she can't see their icons. John, when making a variety of graphics, adds extensions like .psd for Photoshop documents, .eps for the graphic files in the EPS *file format*, .gif for graphics compressed and ready for the web, etc.

Just because you add an extension to a file name doesn't turn that file into that format—you have to create the file in that format in the first place. On the Mac, the extension is simply to identify it to *you*, not to the computer. That is, if you have a graphic you want to put on the web, you can't just add a .gif extension to the end of its name to make it a *GIF* file—you have to create it as a GIF in the first place!

file format
The **file format** refers to how the computer internally sees and understands the file. For instance, to you it might look like a photo on the screen, but to the computer it is a certain file format, either a TIFF, EPS, GIF, or JPEG. Although the external result might look the same, internally each format is very different.

Different file formats are used for different things. For instance, a photograph that will be printed is usually in the TIFF format, but a photo for presentation on the web is usually in the JPEG format. Part of knowing your computer is knowing the different file formats, what they do, and when you would want to use each one.

Finder
The **Finder** is the software that runs the *Desktop*. Please see the definition for Desktop.

FireWire
First, a *bus* is a system of hardware, software, and wiring that lets all the different parts of your computer communicate with each other. **FireWire** is Apple's new trademarked version of a high-performance bus for connecting up to 63 devices through one *port* on a Mac. FireWire is only built into the newest desktop Macs, like the 1999 blue-and-white G3s and up. The iBook does not have a FireWire port at the moment.

GIF **GIF** stands for graphical interchange format and is pronounced "gif," not "jif" because the "g" stands for "graphical." The big thing about the GIF *file format* is that it's *compressed*, which makes it very useful for web graphics. The *extension* is .gif. Typically, GIFs are used for graphics that have flat colors, such as type, drawn illustrations, logos, etc. For photographs, the file format most often used on the web is *JPEG*.

hard copy **Hard copy** refers to the pages you print out, as opposed to the digital copy that is inside the computer or that gets sent as email.

hardware **Hardware** is the stuff you can bump into, like the computer box itself, the monitor, a scanner, a printer, etc.

hard wired When we talk about **hard wired** phones in this book, we mean the kind that are wired directly from the base of the telephone right into the wall. There's no place to plug in your modem cable. You can't separate any of the parts of a hard wired phone like you can with the modular sort of phone with the little connectors that snap into those cute little sockets.

home page A **home page** is to a web site what a table of contents page is to a book. When you type in a web address that ends after the .com or .org part, you end up at the home page. For instance, if you go to www.apple.com, you will get to their home page which will direct you to the rest of the site. If you go to www.apple.com/applescript, you will get to the part of the site that discusses AppleScripting, not to the home page of the Apple site.

Some web sites have an entry page before you get to the home page. The entry page is sort of a welcome mat or the title page in a book; the home page is still the table of contents.

hot key A **hot key** is a key you press that has some special feature programmed into it. Many applications let you assign hot keys to make things happen. For instance, to take a screen shot of something we want to show in this book, we press F13, which is the key we designated as the hot key for that action.

.hqx The *extension* **.hqx** at the end of a file name indicates this file has been compressed specifically for a Macintosh computer in the "binhex" format. This format travels well over networks and can be read even by older machines, whereas the newer format called "binary" with an extension of .bin sometimes can't be read by older machines and software.

HTML HTML stands for Hypertext Markup Language. This is the code used to create web pages. It's pretty simple for code, which is why so many people who have no clue how to design anything can make web pages. You can write the code in a word processor. You can open a page of HTML code in any browser, on any computer, in any web authoring program, and on any word processor. The browser and the web authoring program are the only software applications that will actually interpret the code and display the text and graphics as the author meant them to be.

A web authoring program will let you design web pages without having to write any code—the program writes the HTML code for you.

hub Because the iBook only has one *USB port*, you need to buy a USB **hub** (illustrated to the left) if you want to attach more devices to the computer. The hub, which is generally a little box with extra ports on it, connects to the one USB port, then you can connect four or six or more devices to the hub. You can even connect another hub to the first hub and string up to 127 devices together.

Internet The Internet, which was started in the late 1960s and has been growing ever since, is a system of cables and satellites around the world that lets computers send messages to each other. It's kind of like the electrical wiring system in your house—you can plug in different devices in your house to do different things, but they all use the same wiring system.

One of the things you can do on the Internet is send email. Another thing you can do is *download* files from *servers*. Another is join newsgroups so you can read and post messages about esoteric topics with people around the world on an electronic bulletin board. Another is view web pages and search for information on the World Wide Web. All of these different things you can do all use the same system to send and receive information—the Internet system of connected computers.

intranet An **intranet** is similar to the concept of the Internet, but it's not open to the public. Generally, an intranet is contained within a corporation or university and the information posted on the intranet is for inside users, not for the world at large. Intranets are typically protected from the outside world so you have to have permission to get in.

Jaz drive and disk · A **Jaz drive** is a *peripheral* device (meaning it's something you can add to your computer by plugging it in) that reads small-sized hard disks. The **Jaz disks** are not much bigger than floppy disks, but they can hold one or two gigabytes of data each. Many graphic designers use Jaz disks or at least *Zip disks* for transferring huge graphic files.

JPEG · **JPEG** stands for Joint Photographic Experts Group and is a *compression* file format. Most photographs you see on the web are JPEG files because they are small in file size. Because of the compression, though, JPEGs usually don't look very good when printed.

LAN · **LAN** stands for local area network (as opposed to a *WAN*, or wide area network). A LAN is what you might have in a small office, a school lab, or even at home between a couple of computers. A network is a system of software, hardware, and wires that lets all the different computers in a room or house or small office communicate with each other and send files back and forth. See Chapter 5 about sharing files for directions on how to set up your computers with a simple LAN.

manual dial · When we talk about **manual dialing** in this book, we mean you have to use the fingers on your hand to push the buttons on the telephone, as opposed to *autodialing* where the modem dials the phone internally.

memory (RAM) · **Memory** and hard disk space can be confusing at first. This is the difference: The hard disk is where you store files permanently; it's like your filing cabinet. Memory is where the **computer** stores files as it's working on them; it's like your desk. In your office, you get things out of the filing cabinet to work on them at your desk, then when you're done you put them back into the filing cabinet. That's basically what the computer does.

The bigger your hard disk, the more things you can put it in. The more memory, the more files you can work on at the same time. For instance, with enough memory you can have your web authoring software open to create your web site, the browser Netscape Communicator open so you can check your pages as you create them, and Photoshop open so you can make the graphics for your web pages (that's like having a really big desk). If you don't have enough memory, you have to open one application at a time, then quit that application to have enough room to open another one.

The iBook usually ships with 32 megabytes of RAM (random access memory, the basic kind your computer uses to work). This 32 megs is okay, but it's not a lot, depending on what you plan to do with your iBook. If you do word processing and cruise the web, it will probably be plenty. If you plan to do desktop publishing or graphics, you'll want to add more.

To add more memory to your iBook, call one of the catalogs or memory vendors (see page 192), tell them exactly what kind of computer you have, and they'll send you little memory chips. They're about the size of a stick of gum, and you open the keyboard to your iBook and snap them in. For details on how to do this on your iBook, see Chapter 1.

You'll hear reference to different kinds of memory, such as DRAM (dee ram), SRAM (ess ram), SDRAM, PRAM (pee ram), VRAM (vee ram) and others. They're all memory with slight differences and purposes.

If you're so new to your Mac that you don't really know what memory is, we strongly recommend you read *The Little Mac Book*. We guarantee you will learn a lot and actually enjoy it.

modem The word **modem** is actually a combination of **mod**ulate and **dem**odulate. Most of us have a modem between our computers and the phone, and its job is to take the *digital* information from the computer and turn it into *analog* information that can be sent through the phone lines. The modem on the other end (at the computer where you are sending the data) takes the analog information and turns it back into digital information for the other computer that you're sending the information to.

Your iBook (and many other Macs) has an internal modem instead of a little modem box that sits outside your computer.

If you connect to something that is not the phone line, such as a cable, T1, DSL, or other high-speed digital line, you won't use your modem and modem cable—you'll use the Ethernet cable, which sends the digital information straight to the digital high-speed line.

NNTP **NNTP** stands for network news transfer protocol, which is the system that manages the postings by newsgroups. If you are asked to supply an address for your NNTP, call your Internet service provider and ask them what it is.

operating system (OS) The **operating system** is the software that runs your computer. If you don't have an operating system, your iBook is just a booster seat.

The operating system is what gives a computer its look-and-feel—it controls how the menus open and what they display, the icons, the special features like *contextual menus*, and much more. Operating systems are constantly being updated; they have version numbers just like application software. For instance, today as we write this book we are using Mac OS 8.6 (OS stands for operating system). Tomorrow we might be using OS 9. On PCs, the current operating system is Windows 98.

As operating systems update, software is updated to work with the new features and capabilities, which is why you can't run old software on new systems.

parallel　**Parallel** refers to a certain type of connection on a computer, so you might hear terms like "parallel printer," "parallel cable," or "parallel port." See the definition for *serial.* Your iBook does not have a parallel port of any sort. It uses *USB* connections.

PBX　**PBX** stands for **p**rivate **b**ranch e**x**change. Most hotels and large office buildings have what's called a PBX switchboard, where they have an internal phone center that controls all the extension phones in the building. If you're in a hotel or office building and want to use your modem to connect to the Internet or your home office, you have to get through the PBX system.

Some PBX systems are *digital* and some are *analog.* If it's a digital system, as it is in most new and fancy hotels and office buildings, you can't plug your modem cable into the phone or you'll blow out your modem. See Chapters 8 and 9 for details on getting through a hotel PBX.

PC　Even though the letters **PC** stand for "personal computer," a Macintosh (such as your iBook) is not considered to be a "PC." That's because the term IBM PC was trademarked in the 1970s to apply to computers that used some version of DOS (disk operating system, now monopolized by Microsoft). When the Mac was invented in 1984, it was so phenomenally different from any other computer on earth that personal computers became divided into "PCs" and "Macs." If you told a veteran Mac user you had a PC, thinking in your mind that you mean "personal computer," the Mac veteran would not think you had a Macintosh.

The original Apple computers, such as the Apple IIe, were more like PCs than like Macs.

PC cards, slots　A **PC card** is a little plastic or plastic-and-metal flat piece that slips into a special **PC slot** in some computers. A PC card might be as big as an envelope or as small as a postage stamp. It gives a computer more features and capabilities. A PC card might be a modem, a hard disk that holds digital photos in your digital camera that you can then insert into your Mac, a wireless connection system, or a number of other accessories. Your iBook does not have the standard PC slot, but there is a special place under the keyboard to insert an AirPort card (see Chapter 5).

PCMCIA   *PC cards* used to be referred to as **PCMCIA** cards, but the term PCMCIA is now limited to the Personal Computer Memory Card International Association itself, and the cards and slots are called simply (thank goodness) PC cards and PC slots. You'll still hear lots of people using the term PCMCIA, especially geeks who want to impress you.

peripheral   A **peripheral** is any item (often called a "device") that is outside of the main computer box, but attached to it. Your monitor is actually a peripheral device, and so is your mouse, keyboard, printer, and scanner.

POP, POP3   **POP** stands for point of presence, which is the location of an access point to the Internet, like the one your Internet service provider has that connects you, through them, to the Internet.

POP3 stands for post office protocol, which is the system that directs the incoming email to you.

port   A **port** is a socket, a kind of receptacle, on the back or side of a computer and on *peripheral* devices. A port is different from something like a wall socket in your house in that the information through a port goes in both directions. That is, a wall socket sends power in only one direction, like to a lamp or to the computer to power it up. A port lets information go back and forth between the computer and the device.

This is the symbol for a USB port (left) and the port itself (right).

You'll probably hear about serial ports, parallel ports, SCSI ports, FireWire ports, and others. The only port your iBook has is *USB*.

protocol   The word **protocol** refers to the rules that devices and communcation software packages use when they send information back and forth. The devices at both ends of the communication process must use the same protocol or nothing will happen.

PPP   **PPP** stands for point to point protocol, which is what directs different computers to talk to each other over the network. Particularly it directs your personal computer through the phone line to your Internet service provider. It takes the little packets that the *TCP/IP* makes and forwards them to the Internet.

QuickTime · **QuickTime** is a technology from Apple that lets you see and hear sound, animation, movies, and other multimedia features on your Mac. You, the user, don't really *do* anything with QuickTime—mostly you just want to make sure you have the latest version so any movie clips or other multimedia pieces you find will display and run properly.

RAM · **RAM** stands for random access memory. Please see *memory.*

RJ-11 · **RJ-11** is the name of the standard sort of phone connector you see at the end of your telephone cable in your house and at the end of a regular sort of modem cable. An RJ-11 is considered a "modular" phone connector because if you have that sort of connection, your phone can be separated into modules—the handset, the handset cable, the phone itself, and the cable to the wall jack. You can buy new parts (new modules) and mix and match them.

This is the RJ-11 connector we know and love.

Before the modular system, phones were one complete unit that could not be taken apart. Once it was installed in your house, you didn't have much flexibility about its position. Do you remember those? It's now called a *hard wired* system.

SCSI · **SCSI** (pronounced "scuzzy") stands for Small Computer Systems Interface, but what does that tell you? Well, until very recently, SCSI was the standard system for connecting devices like scanners and extra hard drives to a Mac; it was the standard method for separate parts of the computer system to "interface" or communicate with each other. Your iBook does not have a SCSI connection; the new standard is (at the moment, sigh) *USB.*

.sea · A file with the *extension* **.sea** at the end of its name is what's called a **s**elf **e**xtracting **a**rchive, which means it is a *compressed* file that will uncompress itself if you just double-click on it. You can make an sea (pronounced "ess ee ay") file with the utility StuffIt Deluxe. It's a good format to send to people using Macs if you think they don't have any way to uncompress a regular *.sit* or *.hqx* file. Because the sea is actually a small application, the file size is larger than if you compressed it as a .sit or .hqx.

serial   **Serial** refers to a certain type of connection on a computer, so you might hear terms like "serial port," "serial cable," or "serial printer." A serial connection allows data (information) to be sent back and forth between the computer and another device in single streams (as opposed to a *parallel* connection, where data is sent in two streams, but usually in only one direction at a time). Macs have traditionally used serial ports and serial printers, while PCs have traditionally used parallel ports and parallel printers, which is why you couldn't (until fairly recently) use a PC printer on a Mac.

Now, however, the newest Macs, including your iBook, have neither serial nor cable ports—they use *USB*.

server   A **server** is a computer (usually bigger and faster than average) that stores a lot of files and "serves" them to people who need to use them. For instance, a large corporation or a university might have large servers that have databases of information that various people in different offices need, or the server might be the source that handles all the incoming and outgoing email, or it might have software applications or typefaces that people on different computers can all access at the same time.

Your Internet service provider has servers that you dial into. The server is connected to the Internet 24 hours a day, and serves pages to you. When you create a web site, you send it to a server that serves it to the rest of the world.

.sit   The **.sit** (pronounced "dot sit") you might see at the end of a file name is an *extension* that indicates this file was *compressed*, or "stuffed," using the utility StuffIt Deluxe. You can't really use a .sit file—you must uncompress it, then use the uncompressed file (see *compression*).

software   **Software** refers to the programming code that is either built into your computer or that you buy on disks or download and then install on your computer.

SMTP   **SMTP** stands for simple mail transfer protocol, the system that controls **outgoing** email, that tells it where to go. To receive **incoming** mail, our computers typically use *POP3*. You've probably noticed dialog boxes where you are asked to name your STMP and POP3 accounts.

string You'll often see the word **string** in documentation about modems. In this reference, a string is the series of letters and numbers that tells the modem what to do. This is a typical modem string:

AT7F7C1D27K37Q5E1V1Q0X4^M

synchronize In the context of your iBook, the word **synchronize** means to match the data (information) on one device, such as a PalmPilot, with the data on your iBook. You have Palm Organizer software on your iBook, so if you have a Palm Organize device (a handheld electronic organizer) you can enter dates and meetings and notes in your PalmPilot, then synchronize that with the organizer on your iBook (all it takes is a click of a button, once you set it up the first time), and vice versa so both devices can be updated with current information regularly.

This is a Palm Organizer.

TCP/IP **TCP/IP** is a set of two protocols, or sets of rules, that the Internet uses as its basic communication language to send files from one place to another. You have the TCP/IP program on *your* computer, and every computer you send or receive files from also has the TCP/IP program.

The TCP part (transmission control protocol) takes the message you want to send and splits it into a bunch of little packets. The IP part (Internet protocol) tells the separate packets how to get where they're going—it sends some in this direction and some in that direction. Along the way, the little packets stop at other servers (computers connected to the Internet) and ask directions, and those servers forward the packets along. The TCP on the receiving computer gathers up all the little packets and puts them back together. Amazing.

TIFF **TIFF** stands for Tagged Image File Format. Most digital photographs that are going to be **printed** are in the TIFF *file format* (while most photographs that are going to be seen on the screen, like on the web or in a video presentation are in the *JPEG* format). All of the photos you see in this book are TIFFs.

upload First, *download* means to transfer a copy of a file from another computer to yours. To **upload** means to transfer a copy of a file from your computer to another computer, usually to a *server*. You typically upload a file so someone else can download and use it.

URL The initials **URL** (generally pronounced "you are ell") stand for Uniform Resource Locator, which is a fancy name for a web page address. Every single page on the entire *World Wide Web* has a unique URL. In fact, every single graphic on the web has its own unique URL. You will instantly sound very cool and savvy if you ask somebody what their URL is. This is a typical URL: www.ratz.com.

Url (pronounced "earl") is also the name of the self-proclaimed Internet icon and sex symbol. He has a little buddy named Browser. Visit them at Url's Internet Cafe—go to the URL **www.UrlsInternetCafe.com.**

USB **USB** stands for Universal Serial Bus, the newer connection and data (information) transfer system used on the newest Macs, including your iBook. You plug the mouse, keyboard, printers, scanners, drives, etc., all into the USB ports.

WAN A **WAN** is a wide area network, as opposed to a LAN, which is a small, local area network. A LAN would be used in a situation where all the computers can be physically connected with cables or by a local wireless system, whereas a WAN uses special software and hardware (including satellites or radio waves) to connect computers over a large geographic area.

web page, web site On the *World Wide Web*, everything you see is on a **web page.** A web page is actually, if you look at the code, a page of regular text that tells the *browser* which graphic to display, how big to make the type, which sound to play, etc. You can actually write web pages in a word processor, and you can read them there, if you find that sort of thing interesting.

A collection of web pages for the same company or topic is a **web site**. The main page that acts as a table of contents for the entire site is called the *home page* of the site.

World Wide Web The **World Wide Web** is a technology that allows entire pages filled with graphics, sound, animation, hypertext, movies, etc., to be sent over the *Internet* and viewed on computers. As you surely know, it is changing the world.

Personally, we don't think the web would be here if the Macintosh computer hadn't been invented and changed our expectations of what a computer could do.

Zip drive and disk A **Zip drive** is a *peripheral* device (meaning it's something you can connect to your computer) that reads small-sized hard disks. The **Zip disks** are not much bigger than floppy disks, but they can hold 100 to 250 megabytes of data each. Many graphic designers use Zip disks or *Jaz disks* for transferring huge graphic files. This book was sent to the printer on a Zip disk. They're great.

.zip If you receive a file with the *extension* of **.zip,** the file probably came from a PC. On a Mac, StuffIt Deluxe is the most common file *compression* software and it makes .sit files (as well as .sea or .hqx); on a Windows machine, WinZip is the most common compression software and it makes .zip files. StuffIt Deluxe can unzip zipped files, but that doesn't necessarily mean your iBook can then use the Windows file.

Index

Symbols

.bin, 207
.gif, 206
.hqx, 201, 207
.pdf, 167
.sea, 213
.sit, 201, 214
.zip, 201, 216
10BASE-T, 98
100BASE-T, 98
3Com, 193
3Com Hertz modem, 170

AAUI port, 99
access codes
  in DialAssist, 157
  international dialing, 177
  where to get them, 177
accessories
  acoustic coupler, 147
    cost of, 147
  airplane power adapters, 196
  anti-theft hardware, 188
  auto adapter, 189
  battery charger, 194
  cable, retractable, 146
  cameras, 196
    card reader for digital c., 196
  card readers, 196
  cigarette lighter adapters, 189, 196
  couplers, 145, 146
  digital converters, 145
  doublers, 146, 147
  drives
    floppy, hard, 194
    Zip, 194
  game pads, 194

  hubs, 194
  iBlanket, 181
  IBM Modem Saver, 145
  joysticks, 194
  language translation, 189
  line tester, 145
  list of a. to connect on the road, 170
  microphones, 194
  mouse, 194
  Palm Organizers, 194
  pocket phone, 147
  polarity reverser, 146
  retractable modem cable, 146, 196
  speakers, 194
  surge protectors, 148, 174, 194
  TeleSwitch Plus digital
    converter, 145
  travel bag, 189
  video capture, 194
  video output, 194
  web cams, 196
access point, 32, 112
acoustic coupler
  connect to all phones, 147
  connect to hard-wired phone, 175
  connect to pay phones, 147, 161
  instead of digital converter, 161
  photo of, 147
AC, definition of, 198
AC power adapter, 174
  adjust energy settings for, 23
  better performance with, 20
  C8 connector, two-prong, 148
  illustration of port for, 17
Acrobat
  create PDFs with other Adobe
    software, 167
  Reader included on iBook, 34, 167
Activity Monitor, 109
adapters
  what are they? 198
  AC–DC power adapters, 174
  AccelePort USB-to-serial, 166
  phone jacks, 175

  power plugs, 175
  regional packages of power
    adapters, 152
  USB-to-serial, 166
ADB port, not on iBook, 17
ad hoc network, 113, 114
Adobe
  Acrobat Reader, 167
  products that make PDFs, 167
Agfa, 193
airplanes
  adapter for seatback power
    supply, 196
  how to use phone, 163
  power source on seatback
    adapter to plug iBook into, 196
    DC power, 203
  retractable cables for connecting
    on, 146
AirPort Base Station
  what is it? 32, 111
  access point, 112
  AirPort Card and, 111
  basic process of, 32
  connecting to fast lines, 112
  control strip module with, 113
  cost of, 111
  hardware access point, 112
  illustrations of, 32, 111
  modem in, 112
  price of, 32
  security of, 114
  security software in, 32
  software for, 113
AirPort Card, 32
  access point, 112
  advanced users of, 114
  AirPort Base Station with, 111
  changes Modem control panel
    options, 89
  control strip module, 114
  cost of, 111
  creates a LAN, 113
  disconnect it, 27

iBook will act as base station, 32
illustration of, 32
security of, 114
software access point, 112
software with, 113
where it gets installed, 113
wireless networking with, 113
turn off to conserve battery, 184

airports
avoid the belt in x-ray machine, 187
fax machine at, 187
getting the iBook through
    security, 187
Laptop Lanes, 167, 187
laptops stolen from, 188
printers at, 187
Smart Offices, 167, 187
travel with serial number, 188

AirPower, 187

aliases, 198
for connecting to file sharing, 110

Alt GR keys (alt gr), 72

AltaVista email, 137

alternating current, 198

America Online
explore it, 61
AOL Link makes you crazy, 63
AOLNet to check email around
    the world, 178
as Internet connection, 77
browsed pages appear in
    Internet Explorer History, 60
browser in, 200
buddy list, 119
BYOA (Bring Your Own Access), 63
check email on web, 178
cost of, 75
does not provide finger info, 86
email
    add attachment, 120
    AOLNet to check email around
        the world, 139
    check at Internet cafes, 139
    five screen names available, 119
    make a mailing list, 121
    make new screen names, 119
    read it, 120
    send photo in message, 123
    send to entire mailing list, 121
    shortcut to send, 120
    signature in—make do, 132
    why it disappears in 30 days, 140
    write it, 120
Favorites, 62
    edit, delete, organize, 62
find downloads, 63
go to the Internet, 62
if graphics looks bad, 63

if moving slowly, 63
instant messages, 119
is your ISP and email client, 75, 117
Keywords, 61
log on, 85
    as "Guest," 139
make a mailing list, 121
make an address book, 121
organize email, 122
Personal Filing Cabinet, 122
PictureViewer
    open any graphic image with, 123
prevent large files from
    downloading, 63
traveling with
    check email around the world,
        139, 178
    set up new location, 155
use a different browser, 85
use Netscape browser, 62

AmEx free email, 137

AMPS, 179

analog
data ports, 203
PBX system, 210
vs. digital, 198

animations on web pages; stop, 55

AOL. *See also* **America Online**
what is it? 199

AOLNet
check AOL email on web, 139, 178

Appearance control panel
collapse windows, 53

AppleCD Audio Player, 50–53

Apple, Inc.
find user groups through, 167
web site, 190
    for USB, 192

AppleInsider, 190

Apple menu
apple is flashing with telephone
    pole icon, 85
Network Browser for file sharing, 105
turn file sharing on and off, 109

AppleScript, 199
can program into Fkey, 70

AppleShare extension
necessary for file sharing, 98, 106

AppleTalk
what is it? 98, 149
change network connections via,
    100
file sharing and A., 100
if Options button is not visible, 184
Location Manager tells you it's
    default, 149
make a new configuration, 151

necessary for file sharing, 98
necessary for networking, 106
turn it on or off
    how to, 184
    the preferred way, 100
    to conserve battery, 184
wireless option in, 100

Apple IIe computers, 211

AppleWorks, 34

**applications automatically open
    with Fkey, 70**

appointments in Palm software, 36

APS Tech, 193

archive
definition of, 199
self-extracting, 213

Ariston Technologies, 193

arrow keys, 72, 69

ASCII, 199
pictures in email signatures, 132

askee, 199

AT&T
international calling cards, 177
web site for, 177

attachments
etiquette in sending, 134

audio CDs
change the order of songs, 51
name the songs, 51
play on your Mac, 50

autodialing, 199
does phone accept it? 147, 156
vs. manual dial, 199

Automated Tasks
share a folder, 103
turn file sharing on or off, 109

auto power adapter, 189

AVerMedia, 193

Avid Technologies, 193

B

babelfish, 188

babe magnet, xii

base station, 32. *See also*
    AirPort Base Station

battery
charge time, 31
charger for, 195
charging contacts, 31
conserve b. power, 20, 21
    allow processor cycling, 184
    disconnect external devices, 184
    plug in power supply, 184

processor cycling, 23
quit unused applications, 184
reduce screen brightness, 184
remove CD, 184
sleep, 184
turn off AirPort Card, 184
turn off AppleTalk, 184
use RAM disk, 185
Energy Saver control panel for, 20
Lithium-Ion for iBook, 195
port glows green or amber, 31
recharges when iBook is
plugged in, 17
refusal to charge, 18
replace it, how to, 24
baudy language, 119
beacon light, 23
Belkin Components, 193
Biking Across Kansas, xi
.bin, 207
binary, 207
binhex, 207
bits, 202, 203
blind carbon copy email, 134
bookmarks
tips in Netscape, 56
brb (be right back), 119
Brown, C. Ann, 34
Browser, Url's buddy, 215
browser hand, 54
browsers
what are they? 200
choose default for, 88
default application setting, 88
how to use, 200
set home page, 88
set search page, 88
Browse the Internet, 85, 200
change default browser of, 67
change the browser it defaults
to, 88
default browser for, 88
icon on Desktop, 67
log on to Internet with it, 85
buddy list in AOL, 119
Bugdom, 65
bus, 200, 215
byte, 202, 203

**C5/C6 connector on power supply,
148**
cable modem, 112
use Ethernet, 17
cables
retractable case for, 146, 196
calendar in Palm software, 35, 36
calling cards
faxing with, 43
international, 177
authorization code on, 177
suffix on, 158, 169
using in DialAssist, 157
**call waiting interrupts
connection, 81**
turn it off, 81
cameras
sit on top of computer, 196
USB card reader for, 196
Captivate Select, 70
cards
what are they? 200
camera, 196
Compact Flash, 196
PC cards, 211
SmartMedia, 196
carrying bag for iBook, 189
cats and carpet create static, 26
cat 3 or cat 5, 99
CDs
remove to conserve battery
power, 184
travel with system CD, 186
cell phones
can connect to some
PowerBooks, 170
cannot connect to your iBook,
170
GSM, 179
rent or buy, 179
web site for info, 179
networks in States, 179
networks overseas, 179
using overseas, 179
charging contacts, 31
chat rooms in AOL, 199
Chooser
networking with, 106
use the Network Browser instead,
105
use to share files, 106
CH products, 193

cigarette lighter adapter
airline adapter for, 187
DC power, 203
vendors for, 196
with three outlets, 189
clicking
click-and-a-half, 201
double-click speed, 19
with trackpad, 19
code, html, 207
collapse windows, 53
Command key, 69
commas
example of using, 43
how to use, 42
set length of pause, 42
Compact Flash cards, 196
Compact Pro, 201
compression
what is it? 200
.bin, 207
.hqx, 207
.sea, 213
.sit, 214
.zip, 201, 216
archives and c., 199
Compact Pro, 201
extensions for, 201
GIF files, 206
JPEG files, 206, 208
lossy vs. lossless, 200
schemes of, 200
self-extracting archive, 213
stuffed files, 201
StuffIt Deluxe, 201
StuffIt Expander, 201
CompuCable, 193
Computer Discount Warehouse, 192
configurations, 81
make new one in Remote Access, 91
Connect to...
set default application, 88
connecting
to the Internet, 85
with America Online, 77
two computers for file sharing, 99
Connectix Virtual PC, 72
connectors
RJ-11 port on iBook, 17
USB ports, 17
contextual menus, 201
Control
changes with fn key down, 72
ctrl, 69
Control Buttons, 70

Control key
contextual menus with, 201
illustration of, 71
is a modifier key, 69
control panels
what are they? 202
Appearance, 53
AppleCD Audio Player, 50
AppleTalk
turn off to conserve battery, 184
Date & Time
check after PRAM reset, 24
DialAssist, 91
Energy Saver, 20
File Sharing, 101
File Synchronization, 28
General Controls, 18
Internet, 86, 118
Keyboard, 74
Location Manager, 149
Memory, 185
Modem, 89, 186
explained, 89
Mouse, 19
check after PRAM reset, 24
Remote Access, 90, 158
Speech, 183
TCP/IP, 92
Trackpad, 19
Users & Groups, 104
Web Sharing, 93
control strip
connect to and disconnect from
the Internet, 85
Energy Saver module, 20
illustration of, 20
turn file sharing on or off, 109
use Remote Access to log on, 85
copy centers to print files, 167
Copy with Fkey, 70, 74
country codes
list of international c.c., 173
couplers, 146
acoustic couplers, 147, 161
cost of, 146
photo of, 145
use with line tester, 160
when necessary, 146
cpu, 202
in iBook, 202
crash, fix it, 18
cross-platform fonts on iBook, 68
ctrl, 69
cubicles in airports, 167
current
AC, 198, 203
DC, 198, 203
Cut with Fkey, 70, 74

D-AMPS, 179
data
what is it? 202
data, data port, 145, 202
database, 34
**data connection is Internet
or email, 163**
Date & Time control panel
check after PRAM reset, 24
DC vs. AC, 198
demodulate, 209
desk as memory, 208
DeskJet 340, 166
Desktop
what is it? 203
rebuild it, 186
vs. Finder, 203
DialAssist, 91
details of using, 157–158
in action, 156, 158
must use Advanced User mode, 91
suffixes in, 158
Dialing Settings for FAXstf, 42
dialing, why we call it that, 176
dial manually, 147
in action, 163
dial tones
check for support of autodialing,
156
problem in foreign countries, 176
digital
what is it? 203
data, 202
high-speed lines, 210
modem translates d. to analog, 209
PBX system, 210
vs. analog, 198
digital converter
can use acoustic coupler instead, 161
cost of, 145, 156
in action, 156
line tester to check for current, 145
need for, 145
TeleSwitch Plus, 145
digital phone system
data port on phone, 145
line tester, 145
use acoustic coupler with, 147
use digital converter with,
145, 156
Digital Subscriber Line, 17, 112
direct current, 203

disconnect from file sharing, 109
disconnect from Internet, 85
disks
drives for, 204
hard disks, 208
Jaz, 208
Zip, 216
display, set sleep patterns for, 21
DNS addresses, 82
documents
automatically open with Fkey, 70
domain name, 82
DOS, 211
double-click speed, 19
doublers, 146, 147
connect modem and phone, 76
cost of, 146
foreign travel with, 175
useful when manual dialing, 147
when necessary, 146
downloading
what is it? 203
compressed files, 201
.hqx files, 201
.sit files, 201
.zip files, 201
drag with trackpad, 19
DRAM, 209
draw program, 34
drive bay, 204
driver, 204
drives
what are they? 204
in iBook, 204
Jaz, 208
Zip, 216
DriveSavers, 190
DSL connection, 112
use Ethernet, 17
duplex phone connectors, 175

earl (Url), 215
earphone port, 17
EarthLink
what is it? 64
Alaska and Hawaii are not local, 148
cost for service, 64
email on, 80
international Internet access, 178
is your ISP, 117
local access numbers, 148
needs an email client, 117

Personal Start Page, 80
pricing, 78
set up connectivity with, 78
TotalAccess folder is 63MB, 64
web page examples, 64, 80
EdView Internet Safety Kit, 65
eFax.com, 171
in action, 159
electronic bulletin board, 207
email
address books in, 118
address vs. account, 83
all caps in, 134
America Online
check email on web, 178
bcc (blind carbon copy, 134
chain letters, 134
check it
all accounts at once, 137
any account, 139
at someone else's computer, 126
collect it anywhere in the
world, 137
free accounts at public libraries,
139
choose default e-mail application,
87
contact your ISP when things
go wrong, 117
custom addresses available, 137
deleted from server, 138, 139
don't let it be, 140
domain name, host name, 82
EarthLink, 80
etiquette, 134
file incoming mail, 118
freemail, 137
is not an ISP, 137
Internet Control Panel specs, 87
Internet Explorer, 128
junk mail, 134
how to forward it, 134
send them Url's message, 134
multiple addresses, one account,
118
national providers, 136
Netscape Messenger for, 124
Outlook Express, 128
POP3 accounts, 137, 214
retrieve company email from
anywhere, 138
save it for later, 118, 140
school or office, check it, 117
set default application, 87
set default application for, 118
SHOUTING IN, 134
signatures in, 132

SMTP for outgoing, 214
sounds on receiving, 87
stored on server, 140
turn off call waiting, 81
user name and password, 81
uses Internet, 207
write offline, 118
you need two things, 117
emailaddresses.com, 137
emulation software, 72
encryption
in AirPort wireless network, 114
Encyclopedia, World Book, 34
End key, 72
Energy Saver control panel, 20
Entrega Technologies, 193
Epson, 193
Ethernet
what is it? 98, 204
10/100 Base-T, 98
AAUI ports on older Macs, 99
crossover cable for wireless
network, 32
file sharing through, 99
icon above port, 99
illustration of connector, 17, 204
instead of analog modem, 210
port, 17, 192
RJ-45, 17
vs. phone cable, 76
Excite.com
free email, 137, 172
free voicemail, 172
expansion card, 27
RAM, 26
extensions (file names)
what are they? 205
.bin, 207
.hqx, 201, 207
.sea, 213
.sit, 201, 214
.zip, 201, 216
for compression, 201
extensions (software)
what are they? 204
conflicts with, 204
vs. control panels, 202
Extensions Manager, 205

F

family reunion, xii
Farallon, 111
favorites, 58, 62
faxing
at airports, 187
check these tips, 168
commas
how to use, 42
set length of, 42
Dialing Settings vs. locations, 169
don't connect to the Internet, 168
eFax.com, 171
free faxes on web, 171
in action, 159
hot keys for Print-to-Fax menu, 45
list of accessories for computer, 170
need calling card
international call, 168
long distance call, 168
on the road, 168–169
phonebook for, 49
prefixes, 43
prevent incoming faxes, 44
receiving faxes on iBook, 41, 44
send it!, 49
Smart Dialing locations, 46
software can't tell fax from voice,
44
suffixes, 43
tell modem to wait before
hanging up, 42
tip: call number before faxing, 169
to yourself in hotel, 166
transmittal speed of, 44
use FAXstf software, 41
using calling cards, 43
FAXstf software
Answer On, 44
before sending for the first time, 41
commas
example of using, 43
how to use, 42
set length of pause, 42
Cover Page Settings, 42
Dialing Settings, 42
Fax Menu, 45
Fax Numbers (also called
Phonebook), 49
faxing on the road, 168
if it doesn't pick up a fax, 44
Locations
create new ones, 46–47
examples of, 48
Macro field, 43
Page Header, 45

Phonebook
also called Fax Numbers, 49
numbers in, 168
prefix and suffix, 43
example of using, 43
prevent incoming faxes, 44
send it!, 49
set activation keys, 45
set hot keys, 45
set the settings, 41
Smart Dialing, 46
examples of Locations, 48
vs. Dialing Settings, 43
speaker sounds on or off, 44
Station Message, 45
using calling cards, 43, 168
file formats
what are they? 205
GIF, 206
JPEG, 208
TIFF, 215
FileMaker Pro, 34
file names
extensions at ends of, 205
file server, 101
icons for, 108, 109
file sharing
alias for connecting quickly, 110
can't delete RAM disk while on, 185
change privileges, 109
creates twitching, 108
disconnect from, 109
disconnect users from, 109
extensions and control panels
you need, 98
file server, 101
use alias to connect to, 110
find shared folders with Sherlock,
103
guests can share, 104
icons for shared items, 105
Network Browser
connect to network, 105
make an alias for reconnecting,
110
password, 101
reconnect to, 110
Registered User, 106
share your entire Mac, 103
software needed, 98
through Personal Web Sharing, 93
turn it on or off, 101, 109
File Sharing control panel, 101
disconnect individual users, 109
how to share files using, 98
name your Mac for sharing, 101
necessary for file sharing, 98
Program Linking, 101
turn file sharing on or off, 109

File Sharing extension
necessary for file sharing, 98
File Sharing Library
necessary for file sharing, 98
File Synchronization, 28
automating process, 29
destination file, 29
filing cabinet as hard disk, 208
Finder, 205
vs. Desktop, 203
finger, 86
Fire Ants, 65
firewall, 138
FireWire, 205
Fkeys
what are they? 69, 70
what they do, 70
Control Button mode, 70
illustration of, 71
latches in Fkey row, 26
light glow in row, 26
screw in Fkey row, 26
stickers for identifying, 71
use to cut, copy, paste,
and undo, 74
user-defineable, 70
fn key
what is it? 70
illustration of, 71
numeric keypad access, 73
turns into Enter key in AOL, 120
folders
find shared ones, 103
happy faces on, 108
share them, 102
shared, 103, 108
wires coming out of them, 103
fonts
best for web browsing, 57
cross-platform, 68
installed on iBook, 68
TrueType, 68
foreign travel
access codes for calling cards, 177
adapters for power supply, 174
adapters for phone jacks, 175
America Online, access email
from web, 178
checklist for, 180
digital converter for, 176
digital phone systems, 176
EarthLink, 178
find a local Internet service
provider, 179
get a web-based freemail
account, 137
get access numbers before you
leave, 178

GRIC (global roaming access), 178
GSM and cell phones, 179
guide to connectors, codes, etc.,
173
ignore dial tone, 176
iGo resource, 173
international calling cards, 177
international Internet access, 178
language translation software,
189
language translation web site, 188
line filter for tax impulsing, 176
line tester, 145, 146, 156
MindSpring, 178
Mobile Connectivity Guide, 173
modem doesn't recognize tdial
tone, 176
phone surcharges, 178
power adapter for, 174
power plug adapters, 175
pulse phone lines, 176
Remote Access for, 179
reverse polarity, 176
surge protector, 174
tax impulsing, 176
tech support for, 144, 180
TeleAdapt resource and training,
173
forward junk mail properly, 134
freeze, fix it, 18
Function Key
is fn key, 70, 74
function keys. *See* Fkeys
Function Key Settings, 74

G

G3 (blue-and-white)
100BASE-T connections, 98
games need lower screen
resolution, 190
Gates, Bill, 200
General Controls
turn off warning, 18
.gif, 206
GIF
what is it? 206
how to pronounce, 206
gigabyte, 202
glasses icon, 102
global roaming, 136
glossary, 197
extensive g. at whatis, 197
graphics fine-tune the tracking
speed for, 19

GRIC
contact information, 178
GRICtraveler, 152
Network Alliance, 152
partner with MindSpring, 178
Griffin Technologies, 193
GSM
and cell phones, 179
different in States, 179
guest file sharing, 104

h-menus, 202
hard copy, 206
hard disk
set sleep patterns, 21
vs. memory, 208
hardware, 206
hardware access point, 112
hardwired phones
what are they? 206
tool kit for connecting to, 175
vs. modular, 213
headphone jack, 17
Help menu
AppleCD Audio Player Guide, 53
Internet, 96
Location Manager, 151
Palm Desktop documentation, 40
Hertz of power supply, 174
Hewlett-Packard, 193
hierarchical menus, 202
h-menus, 202
home base is the Desktop, 203
Home key, 72
Home Page, 88
home page, 206, 216
host name, 82
hotels
autodialing, does phone accept, 147
digital phone systems in, 145
data port on phone, 145
PBX in, 210
Hot Function Keys, 70, 74
hot keys, 206
change Print option to Fax, 41
to startup new Location, 150
use Fkeys for, 70
HotSync for Palms, 28, 40
HP DeskJet 340, 166
.hqx, 201, 207

HTML, 207
http://, you don't have to type it, 54
hubs, USB, 17, 207
hypertext markup language, 207
Hz, 174

I-beam, make it thicker, 19
IBM Modem Saver
in use, 145, 146
IBM PC, 210
iBook
drive bays in, 204
drives in, 204
hub for, 207
USB port in, 212
iBook Zone, 190
icons
AppleShare, 105
file sharing, 108
glasses icon, 102
on Desktop, what are they? 67
pencil, 102
server icon for sharing, 105
identity module, 179
ignore dial tone, 81, 176
in action, 163
in fax software, 42
iGo
airline adapter for planes, 187
anti-theft hardware, 188
as resource for, 192
cell phones overseas, 179
checklist for foreign travel, 180
contact information, 180
has the answers, 144
LapTraveler for car, 189
line filter for tax impulsing, 176
regional packages of adapters, 152
resource for foreign travel, 173
Socket Multiplier, 189
surge protectors, 174
Illustrator, can make PDFs, 167
iMaccessories, 193
iMacs, 100BASE-T connections, 98
Imation, 193
iName free email, 137
InDesign can make PDFs, 167
Info Center, Mac OS, 67
Infowave Software Inc., 193
input and output connectors, 17
Insignia SoftWindows, 72

Interex, 193
Internet
what is it? 207
connect to, 85
disconnect from, 85
automatically, 90
intranet is not the Internet, 94
IP address, 93
log on or off, 85
protocol, 93
turn off call-waiting before connecting, 81
vs. intranet, 94
Internet Cafe Guide **(booklet), 139**
Internet cafes
how to find them, 139
in action, 160
Internet Cafe Guide (booklet), 139
web site address for, 139
Internet Config, 126
Internet control panel, 86
E-mail settings, 87
finger information, 86
make new set of settings, 86
News settings, 87
newsgroup reader, 87
Personal settings, 86
set default email application, 118
signature, 86
Web settings, 88
Internet Explorer
what is it? 58
bookmarks, called Favorites, 58
Favorites, 58
tab, 58
tips for using, 59
History
tab, 58
tips on using, 60
is a browser, 200
Page Holder, 59
tab, 58
panels on, 58
resize panels, 59
resize text on web page, 58
Search tab, 58
tabs on, 58
uses Outlook Express for email, 58
Internet protocol, 215
Internet service providers
what are they? 75
establish a relationship, 77
find local provider, 75, 136
find one in the world, 179
options for, 75
register with ISP through the Internet Setup Asst., 77
servers at, 214
The List, 136

Internet Setup Assistant, 77
before you begin, 77
fills in Remote Access info, 90
find it, 76
icon for, 77
where to find, 77
print all the data you entered, 84
when to use it, 77

intranet, 208
personal web sharing on, 94
retrieve company email from
anywhere, 138
vs. Internet, 94

IP address, 82, 92
what is it? 93, 95
find it for your computer, 95

ISPs. *See also* **Internet Service
Providers**
find all over the world, 179
find local provider, 136
options for, 75
The List, 136, 179

Iyengar, Rada, iv

Japanese cell phone network, 179
Jaz drive, 208
JPEG, JPEG photos
what is JPEG? 208
don't look great printed, 123
PictureViewer
open any graphic image with,
123
vs. GIF, 206

junk mail
at least forward it properly, 134
send them Url's message, 134

Kansas, Biking Across, xi
Kawasaki, Guy, 198
Kensington, 193
keyboard
control panel for, 74
delay the repetition of characters,
74
illustration of, 71
lock k. shut, 74
remove for RAM installation, 26
replace disconnected k., 27
screw between F4 and F5, 74
triangle above Power button, 18

keyboard shortcuts
arrow keys as edit keys, 72
change screen brightness, 70
change speaker volume, 70
Fkeys for cut, copy, paste, undo, 70
mute speaker, 70
play audio CDs, 52
rebuild the Desktop, 186
reset iBook, 18
restart from system CD, 186
restart iBook, 18
screen shots, 84
send email in AOL, 120
stickers for Fkeys, 71
turn on num lock, 70

Keyspan, 193
kilobyte, 202
Kinko's, 162, 167
Kodak, 193

LaCie, 193
LAN, 77
what is it? 113, 208
example of, 98
vs. WAN, 208
with AirPort Card, 32

language translation, 188, 189
Laptop Lane, 167
LapTraveler, 189
Larsen, Ernst, 139
Lawrence, Joseph, xii
Lawrence, Sarah, xii
lights
beacon to indicate sleep, 23
Num Lock, 26
power port glows green or
amber, 31
screw, 26

line tester
cost of, 145, 156
IBM Modem Saver, 145
illustration of, 145
in action, 156
need for, 145
overcurrent in phone system, 145
reverse polarity, 145
use coupler to connect to cable, 160

links in browser
indicated by hand or underline, 54

links in File Synchronization
change direction in file synch, 29
files to synchronize, 28

local area network, 77, 98
what is it? 113
example of, 98

LocalTalk, 98, 100

Location Manager
choose a location on startup, 150
for more help, 151
yells at you about "Default," 151
how to use, 149

Locations
Smart Dialing (faxing), 46

logging on or off the Internet, 85
log in name, 82
Logitech, 193
long distance numbers
commas in, 157

lossless, 201
lossy, 201
low-quality phone lines, 162
Lucas web site, xii

MacAddict, 190
Macally, 193
MacCentral Online, 190
MacConnection, 192
MacHome Interactive, 190
Macintosh News Network, 190
MacInTouch, 190, 192
resource for products, 192

MacMall, 192
Mac OS Info Center, 67
Macro field
example of, 169
phone card number in, 169
example of in use, 161

Mac User Groups, how to find, 166
MacWarehouse, 192
MacWeek, 190
Macworld Online, 190
mail transfer protocol, 214
MailCity free email, 137
Mail icon
what is it? 67
choose default email client,
67, 87, 88
what it opens, how to change it,
118

mailing list
in AOL, 121
in Netscape Messenger, 125
in Outlook Express, 130

MailStart free email, 137
manual dial, 208
　vs. autodial, 199
McCormack, Korey, iv
McFly, Rollie, 65
MCI
　international calling cards, 177
　web site for, 177
memory
　what is it? 209
　preserve m. contents on sleep, 23
memory chip, 26
Memory control panel, 185
microphone for iBook, 195
Microsoft, 200
　DOS, 211
　Internet Explorer, 58
　Outlook Express, 128
　Word, numeric keypad moves
　　cursor, 73
Microtech Intl., 193
Microtek, 193
MindSpring
　800 number access, 160
　email provider, national, 136
　GRIC partnership, 178
　GRICtraveler, 152
　in action with Url, 155
　international Internet access, 178
　local access numbers, 148
　use Remote Access to call, 158
Modem control panel
　choose "pulse" in some foreign
　　countries, 176
　choose slower connection for
　　noisy phones, 162
　explained, 89
　ignore dial tone, 176
　　in action, 163
　leave sound on, 163
　what to do with it, 89
　use slower connection speed, 186
modems
　what are they? 209
　AirPort Base Station m., 112
　autodialing
　　dial manually instead, 147
　cable for, 17
　danger of digital phones, 145
　don't recognize the dial tone, 176
　drops the connection regularly, 162
　Ethernet connections and, 17
　noisy phone lines, 186
　PBX and m., 203
　phone cable vs. Ethernet cable
　　for, 76
　port on iBook, 17

prevent damage by digital system,
　156
retractable cables for, 196
RJ-11 port on iBook, 17
script for, 82
string, 214
tax impulsing causes problems, 176
to connect cell phone, 170
use data port, 203
use slower connection, 186
modem script, 89
modifier keys
　what are they? 69
　affected by fn key, 72
modular phone
　RJ-11 connector, 212
　vs. hard wired, 206
modulate, 209
moon and stars button, 20
Mouse control panel, 202
　adjust settings, 19
　check after PRAM reset, 24
Mouse Tracks, 19
My Own Mail freemail, 137

N

N-AMPS, 179
Netcom, 136
Netscape
　what is it? 54
　Address Book, 54
　best fonts for web browsing, 57
　bookmarks
　　edit them, 56, 57
　　in toolbar, 54
　　organize them, 56
　　send them all to one folder, 56
　　tips, 56
　Communicator
　　what is it? 200
　　vs. Navigator, 118
　Composer, 54
　connection icon, 54
　create signature, 132
　enter web address, 54
　fixed-width font, 57
　free email, 137
　Inbox, 54
　lock icon, 54
　Messenger (email), 124
　　check your mail at another
　　　desk, 126
　　create mailing list, 125
　　make address book, 125
　　make new message, 125

　　redesign window, 125
　　resize panels in window, 124
　Navigator, 54
　　email client for, 118
　　vs. Communicator, 118
　Newsgroups, 54
　open a new window with a link, 56
　pointer hand, 54
　Preferences, 57, 126
　profiles in, make new ones, 127
　quick search in Location box, 54
　shortcuts for navigating, 55
　stop animations, 55
　toolbars
　　rearrange them, 55
　　roll them up, 55
　uncheck "Internet Config," 126
　user profiles, 124
　　how to make, 127
　variable width font, 57
　"What's Related," 55
network
　what is it? 208
　news transfer protocol, 210
　NNTP, 210
　wake iBook automatically, 23
Network Alliance, GRIC, 152
Network Browser
　connect file sharing with, 105
　make an alias for reconnecting, 110
network news transfer protocol, 210
networking
　AppleTalk, 98
　connecting
　　two computers for file sharing, 99
　　with Chooser, 106
　　with Network Browser, 105
　disconnecting, 109
　Ethernet, 98
　file sharing on several Macs, 98
　find shared folders, 103
　Internet vs. intranet, 94
　LAN, local area network, 98
　LocalTalk, 98
　security of wireless n., 114
　setting up guest users, 104
　share files through personal web
　　sharing, 93
　TokenTalk, 98
　WAN, wide area network, 94
　zones, 106
Newer Technology, 193
newsgroups, 207
　host for, 83
　Outlook Express is good choice, 87
nm/u (not much, you?), 119
NNTP, 210

noisy phone lines, 186
  change modem script, 162
Nokia cell phone to connect
    to computer, 170
Norrena, Jimbo, 62
numeric keypad, 73
  disable all characters except
    keyboard, 73
Num Lock
  fn settings and, 74
  to disable characters, 73
  turn on with Fkey, 70

O

OEMs, 193
on and off signals, 203
ones and zeros, 202
operating system, 34, 210
  versions of, 210
Original Equipment
    Manufacturers, 193
OS, what is it? 210
Outlook Express, 128
  address book in, 130
  as newsgroup reader, 87
  contacts, 130
  email inbox, 128, 129
  Internet Explorer uses as email
    client, 128
  multiple accounts, 131
  signatures in, 133
  switch to another account, 131
overcurrent
  check for with line tester, 145, 156
  problems for modem, 145

P

packets, 92, 215
Page Down key, 71, 72
Page Holder, 59
PageMaker, 73
  can make PDFs, 167
  numeric keypad moves cursor, 73
Page Up key, 71, 73
paint program, 34
Palm Desktop Organizer, 35
  customize it, 39
Palm Organizer
  accessory, 194
  HotSync with iBook data, 28
  photo of, 214
  synchronize with software, 40, 214

paperclip, reset iBook with, 18
parallel, 210
parallel ports
  connect to USB, 192
password, 81
  change it for file sharing, 106
  email and ISP passwords are not
    the same, 82
  file sharing, 101
  guest does not need one, 106
  protection for laptop data, 188
Paste, 134
  with Fkey, 70, 74
pay phones
  acoustic coupler, 147, 161
PBX
  what is it? 210
  data ports to avoid, 202
PC card, 200, 211
PCI bus, 200
PCMCIA, 211
PCs
  what PC means, 210
  compressed files on, 201
  parallel ports on, 213
  vs. Macintosh, 210
  .zip files, 201
PC slot, 211
PC slots
  modem to connect cell phone, 170
PDA, 194
PDC cell phone network in Japan, 179
PDF, 34, 167
pee ram, 24
peer-to-peer networks, 113, 114
pencil icon, 102
peripheral
  what is it? 211
Personal Digital Assistants, 194
Personal Filing Cabinet in AOL, 122
Personal Web Sharing
  what is it? 93
  best suited for intranet, 94
  control panel for, 93
  how to do it, 94
  intranet vs. Internet, 94
pg up, pg dn, 71
phone cables, retractable, 146
phone connectors
  adapters for foreign countries, 175
  couplers, 145, 146
  doublers, 146
  duplex, 175
  list of international c., 173
  modular, 175

RJ-11, 175
  illustration of, 175
  simplex, 175
phone cards
  suffixes on, 158, 169
  using in DialAssist, 157
phones
  autodialing, 156
  beeps regularly, 176
  dial tones
    check for support of
      autodialing, 156
    problem in foreign countries, 176
  digital phone system, 176
  hardwired
    what is it? 206
    in foreign countries, 175
    tool kit for connecting, 175
  low-quality phone lines, fix, 162
  pulse lines, 176
photographs
  JPEG format, 123, 208, 215
  send in AOL email, 123
  TIFF format, 215
Photoshop can make PDFs, 167
Picture 1, 84
PictureViewer
  make an alias of it, 66
  open any graphic image with, 123
PIN
  enter in DialAssist, 158
  enter in fax software, 43
  international calling cards, 177
PlayList, 51
NetAddress free email, 137
PO Box free email, 137
pocket phone, 147
point of presence, 211
point-to-point protocol, 90, 212
pointer
  trail of pointers, 19
polarity, reversed, 160
polarity reverser device, 146
  cost of, 146
POP, 211
POP3, 211
  check with freemail accounts, 137
  retrieve company email, 138
POP Mail, 137
portable document format, 167
ports
  what are they? 211
  AAUI port, 99
  data ports for modems, 145
  Ethernet vs. modem, 76

FireWire, 206
headphone, 17
modem vs. Ethernet, 76
not on iBook, 17
on iBook, 17
parallel, 210
power port, 17
SCSI, 213
serial, 213
USB, 17, 211
　hub for, 207
　illustration of, 211
　vs. wall sockets, 211
post office protocol, 211
power adapters
AC–DC, 174
C8 connector on, 148
Hertz of iBook's, 174
specifications of, 174
surge protector on, 148
voltage of iBook's, 174, 152
PowerBook
connect to cell phone for
　Internet access, 170
power plugs
adapters for foreign travel, 175
list of international p.p., 173
power port, 17
illustration of, 17
power sources
AC, DC, 203
power supply
AC vs. DC, 198
tips to conserve battery, 184
PPP, 90, 212
use TCP/IP control panel, 92
PRAM, 24, 209
prefixes
what are they? 157
commas in, 157
for faxing, 47
using in DialAssist, 157
vs. suffix, 169
printers
DeskJet 340, portable, 166
needs drivers, 204
portable, 166
printing
at airports, 187
copy centers, 167
fax to yourself in hotel, 166
Kinko's, 167
PDF files for, 167
to service bureaus, 166
private branch exchange, 210
processor, 202

processor cycling, 23
Program Linking, 101
ProntoMail free email, 137
protocol
what is it? 212
Internet p. (IP), 215
mail transfer p., 214
on the Internet, 93
point-to-point p., 90
POP, POP3, 212
POP3, 137
PPP, 212
transmission control p. (TCP), 215
**public libraries provide Internet
　access, 139**
pulse phone lines, 176
settings for, 42

QuickTime
what is it? 66, 212
PictureViewer, 66
　make an alias of it, 66
Player, 66
　icon on Desktop, 67
Plugin, 66
Updater, 66
QuickTime PictureViewer, 123

**radio frequencies in wireless
　networking, 111**
RAM, 208
installing, 26
　illustration of, 27
maximum in iBook, 26
shield covering for, 27
using a RAM disk, 185
vs. hard disk, 208
RAM disk
how to create one, 185
how to remove one, 185
random access memory, 209.
　See also RAM
read-only, 102
read-write privileges, 102, 103
RealPlayer, 172
rebuild the Desktop, 186
Reckonwith, Amanda, 62
reconnect to file sharing, 110
reminders from Palm software, 37

Remote Access
can connect with control panel, 90
DialAssist, 158
　in action, 156, 158
dial manually, 163
how to use it, 90
in action, 154
Location Manager doesn't like
　default, 149
make a new configuration, 91, 151
Status bar, 85
　log on to Internet, 85
use control strip module, 159
Remote Access Status, 85
reset
key combination for, 18
turn off warning, 18
**resolution at 640x480
　looks blurry, 190**
restart
from system CD, 186
key combination for, 18
turn off warning, 18
resurrect your data, 190
retractable cables, 196
cost of, 146
reverse polarity
fixing it in action, 160
line tester for, 146
　use coupler to connect to cable,
　160
Polarity Reverser accessory, 146
wires in reverse order, 176
won't harm modem, 146
Reyes, Steve, iv
Right Control, 71
Right Shift, 71
RJ-11
what is it? 212
duplex adapters for, 175
photo of, 17, 212
port on iBook, 17
retractable cable, 146
simplex adapters for, 175
RJ-45
Ethernet, 17
illustration of connector, 17
RocketMail free email, 137
Rohr, Dave, xi
roll up windows, 53
rt crtl key, 71

Santa Fe Screenwriting Conference, 128
scanning in File Synchronization, 30
Schedule, 22
screen
  change brightness with Fkey, 70
  follow movement of pointer, 19
  in broad daylight, 111
  reduce brightness to conserve
    battery, 184
  resolution at 640 looks blurry, 190
  set sleep patterns, 21
screen shots
  how to make, 84
  Captivate Select to make, 70
SCSI, 213
  no port on iBook, 17
  ports, connect to USB, 192
scuzzy, 213
SDRAM, 209
.sea, 213
Search Page in Internet Explorer, 88
search web
  quick search in Netscape
    Location bar, 54
  "What's Related" in Netscape, 55
security
  firewall, 138
  laptops stolen from airports, 188
  password protection, 188
  travel with serial number, 188
security software in AirPort, 32
self extracting archive, 213
serial adapters, 166
serial number in case of theft, 188
serial ports, 213
  connect to USB, 192
  no port on iBook, 17
server
  what is it? 213
  in file sharing, 101
  stores your email, 140
**service bureaus might print
  your pages, 166**
SFeSC, 128
**shared folders, find with Sherlock,
  103**
sharing files. *See also* file sharing
  folder icons for, 103
  icons for shared items, 105
  info dialog box box, 102
  share your entire Mac, 103

**sharing iBook, use Location
  Manager, 149**
Sherlock
  use it to find shared folders, 103
shut down
  automatically, 22
signatures in email, 132
  America Online kludge, 132
  Internet control panel, 86
  Outlook Express, 133
simple mail transfer protocol, 214
simplex adapter, 175
.sit, 201, 214
site, web site, 216
Skyline Wireless PC Card, 111
sleep
  what is it? 20
  beacon light to indicate s., 23
  conserve battery, 184
  control it, 20
  get through airport security
    faster, 187
  preserve memory contents, 23
  set it up, 20
  set separate settings for display
    and hard disk, 21
  wake up options, 23
    iBook automatically when
      opened, 23
Small Dog Electronics, 192
Smart Dialing, 46
  entering data for Locations, 47
  examples of Locations, 48
  using a Macro, 169
SmartMedia cards, 196
Smart Offices, 187
SMTP, 214
SMTP host, 83
socket vs. port, 212
Socket Multiplier, 189
software
  what is it? 214
  old s. won't run on new OS, 210
  what's included on iBook, 33
software access point, 112
SoftWindows, 72
sounds
  change level of with Fkey, 70
  on receiving email, 87
speaker, built-in
  change volume with Fkey, 70
  mute it with Fkey, 70
speakers for iBook, external, 195

Special
  at the Desktop or Finder, 203
Speech control panel, 183
speech recognition
  ViaVoice speech recognition, 195
speed
  double-click s., 19
  tracking s., 19
spreadsheet, 34
spring-loaded folders, 201
Sprint
  international calling cards, 177
  web site for, 177
SpryNet, 136
SRAM, 209
startup iBook automatically, 22
Startup Items Folder
  remove Web Sharing alias, 95
static electricity
  can freeze computer, 18
  discharge on metal, 27
  when replacing battery, 26
stickers for Fkeys, 71
storage media
  Compact Flash card, 196
  SmartMedia card, 196
string, 214
studio x, 83
stuffed files, 201
StuffIt Deluxe, 216
  .sit file from, 214
StuffIt Expander, 201
suffixes
  in calling cards, 158
surge protectors
  accessory, 195
  cost of, 148
  need to replace, 148
  portable ones, 148
switchboard, PBX, 210
synchronize files, 28
  automating process, 29
  destination file, 29
  master file, 29
  two-way synch, 29
**synchronize iBook data
  with Palm, 214**
**system software CD,
  restart with, 186**

T

T1 line, 112
Talking Alerts, 183
talking voice, turn it off, 183
tax impulsing, 176
TCP/IP
 how does it work? 214
 what is it? 92
 Location Manager doesn't like
  the default, 149
 make a new configuration, 151
 what TCP/IP does, 92
 works with PP, 212
TeleAdapt
 acoustic coupler, 175
 airline adapter for planes, 187
 AirPower Database, 187
 anti-theft hardware, 188
 as resource, 192
 cell phones overseas, 179
 checklist for foreign travel, 180
 contact information, 174, 180
 digital converter, 156
 has the answers, 144
 line filter, 176
 Mobile Connectivity Guide, 173
 Regional Power Packs, 152
 resource for foreign travel, 173
 retractable cables, 146
 surge protectors, 174
 tech support 24/7, 144, 180
 TeleSwitch Plus, 145
 thanks to, iv
 which airline seats have power, 187
telecommunications software,
 34, 90
TeleSwitch Plus, 145
 cost of, 145
10 or 100BASE-T connections, 98
terabyte, 202
text only, 199
text clipping, 132
thatweb.com, 139
theft of laptops, 188
 travel with serial number, 188
The List, 136, 179
thick I-beam, 19
Thomas, Jimmy
 graduation site, xii
 Lucas site, designed by, xii
Thornton, Elizabeth, 164
TIFF, 215
Timberland laptop bag, 189

Tollett, John, 164
 connecting on plane, 146
 The Non-Designer's Web Book, 95
tracking speed, 19
trackpad
 click and drag with, 19
 control panel to adjust, 19
 Mouse control panel and, 19
transceiver, 99
Translation Experts Limited, 189
translation software, 188, 189
traveling
 why travel with iBook, 154
 acoustic coupler, 161
 adapters
  for airplane seatback, 196
  for auto, with three outlets, 189
  for foreign countries, 175
 car travel, 189
  passenger seat desk, 189
 data port in hotel phones, 145
 digital converter
  in action, 156
  need for, 145, 156
  use acoustic coupler instead, 161
 email
  access AOL email, 178
  check thatweb.com, 139
  free email on web, 137
 faxing with calling cards, 46
 find Internet service providers all
  over the world, 179
 find the local Mac User Group, 167
 foreign countries
  checklist for, 180
  guide to connectors, codes,
   etc., 173
 hotels
  autodialing, does phone accept,
   147
  phone systems, 145
 Internet Cafe Guide (booklet), 139
 language translation software,
  188, 189
 Laptop Lanes in airports, 167
 line filter for tax impulsing, 176
 line tester
  check for digital line, 145
  check for reverse polarity, 146
  in action, 156
 overcurrent in phone system, 145
 power plug adapters, 175
 print at Kinko's, 167
 public libraries provide Internet
  access, 139
 retractable phone cable, 146
 reverse polarity, 176

 save email to pick up later, 140
 set up Remote Access before
  you go, 154
 theft of laptops, 188
 travel bags for iBook, 189
 with Url, 153
triangle printed on iBook, 18
troubleshooting
 DriveSavers for emergencies, 190
 iBook won't pick up fax, 44
 rebuild the Desktop, 186
 remove alias of Web Sharing, 95
 unreliable modem connection, 186
 use system CD to restart, 186
TV, presentations to from iBook,
 194
twisted pair, 99
twitches while file sharing, 108
two-prong AC adapter, 148
typing, too many characters
 repeat, 74

U

Umax Technologies, 193
Undo with Fkey, 70, 74
Universal Serial Bus, 215. *See* **USB**
unstuff files, 201
upload, 215
URL, what is it? 215
Url Ratz
 who is he? xi, 215
 at the office, 13
 filing junk mail, 134
 mean trick he suggests, 183
 on a road trip with, 153
 Road Hog, 141
 waiting for a phone, 164
Url's Internet Cafe
 glossary at, 197
 meet Url, 215
 message re junk mail, 134
USB
 what is it? 215
 adapters to connect non-USB
  devices, 192
 cameras, 196
 compatibility of devices, 17
 floppy drives for, 195
 game pads, 194
 hard drives for, 195
 hub for, 17, 194, 207
 joysticks, 194
 mouse for iBook, 194
 port, illustrated, 17

presentation hardware, 194
printers, 194
resources for products, 192
scanners, 194
SuperDisk floppy drives, 195
ViaVoice headset, 195
video capture, 194
Zip drives for, 195
user-definable Fkeys, 70
user name and password, 81
user profiles, 127
Users & Groups
for file sharing, 98, 104

v.34, v.90, 162
ViaVoice headset, 195
video cameras, 194
video output, 194
Virtual PC, 72
Virtual Private Network, 152
voice that speaks the alerts,
turn it off, 183
voicemail, free on the web, 172
voltage in DC, 203
voltage transformer for iBook
is unnecessary, 152
VPN, 152
VRAM, 209

Wacom, 193
wake up iBook
automatically when opened, 23
control it, 20
options for, 23
WAN, 215
Internet access and, 94
vs. LAN, 215
warning
turn it off, 18
web addresses
IP address, 93
URLs, 215
web authoring program, 207
web cams for iBook, 196

web pages
what are they? 216
create them in Composer, 54
displayed by browser, 200
make text larger, 58
safety kit for kids, 65
stop animations in Netscape, 55
Web Sharing control panel, 93, 94
example of using, 94
remove alias from Startup Items
folder, 95
what to do with it, 93
wide area network, 94
Williams, Cliff, 47, 123
Williams, Julie, 123
Williams, Prairie, 123
Williams, Robin, 164
connecting on plane, 146
daughter, Scarlett, 119, 164
son, Jimmy Thomas, xii
Williams, Scarlett, 119, 164
Williams, Trevor, 123
Windows
emulation software on the iBook,
72
Menu key, 72
SoftWindows, 72
Start menu, 72
Windows key, 72
WinZip, 216
windows on iBook, collapse them, 53
Winstation, 193
WinZip, 216
wireless networking
AirPort Base Station, 111
AirPort Card and, 111
connect wired computers to, 111
security of, 114
switch between networks, 113
to share files, 99
word processor, 34
Word Translator, 189
World Book Encyclopedia, 34
World Wide Web
what is it? 216
connect or disconnect, 85
uses Internet, 207
write only, 102

Yahoo
find ISPs, 136
free email, 137
you are ell, 215
"You've Got Mail," 87

.zip, 201, 216
Zip drive, 216
add to iBook, 204
zones, 106

Fonts used:
Kumquat for the chapter heads
and numbers
Bell for body copy
Officina Sans for the bold sans serif

Software: PageMaker 6.5

Checklist

To connect to the Internet or send a fax while on the road, you'll probably run into a wide variety of telephones—digital, pay phones, PBX switchboard systems, airline satellite connections, etc. Before you leave home, read Chapter 8 to learn all about the extra devices you need for making a phone connection away from home. We recommend, at a bare minimum, that you take these items along (prices are approximate):

- **Phone jack doubler** (available in office supply stores, $5)
- **Phone cable coupler** (available in office supply stores, $5)

   The following items (as well as the items above) are available through **www.teleadapt.com** and **www.iGo.com.**

- **Portable surge protector,** which you should use at home anyway ($20)
- **Line tester** to test the phone lines to see if they are digital (which will blow up your modem) and if the polarity is reversed (which won't hurt your modem, but you probably won't connect) ($30)
- **Polarity reverser** in case the wires in the phone line are crossed ($15)
- **Digital converter** to connect to digital hotel and office phone systems or you'll destroy your modem ($140)
- If you plan to connect from pay phones, you'll need an **acoustic coupler** ($130). The acoustic coupler can be very handy because it will also work on digital phone systems so you wouldn't need a digital converter.

There are lots of other great tools you can take along, but these will get you through most situations in North America. If you're leaving the country, read Chapter 11 because you'll need several other items.

Final Thoughts

When Peachpit Press approached Robin about writing *The Little iBook Book*, she offered me the opportunity to co-author the book with her (actually, says Robin, I told John that I didn't want to write it, but if he wanted to do it, I would help), and suggested we include Url Ratz, the self-appointed Internet icon that runs UrlsInternetCafe.com. I had doubts that this was a good idea, but I've seen Robin's unorthodox approach work before. I mean, who else would title a computer book *The Mac is not a typewriter?* Who else could convince their publisher that the "book level" designation of a book should be "beginnerish" instead of "beginner"? And now a rodent? Well, it's that kind of down-to-earth fun and freshness that made this book so much fun to work on, in addition to the fabulous iBook itself.

I could say more about Robin, but I'll be surprised if she doesn't delete what I've already said. So I'll just say that working with Peachpit Press on *The Little iBook Book* was the quintessential writer/publisher experience. Our thanks and gratitude to everyone there for their expertise, trust, and support.

With this crew—and the iBook—we would be pretty worried about ourselves if we hadn't had fun.

We look forward to seeing you all "on the road."

John (and Robin and Url)